APOCALYPTIC BODIES

Apocalypse can be broadly defined as any representation of the end of the world or anxiety over and preparation for the end of time. In this timely volume, Tina Pippin traces the biblical notions of end times as represented in ancient and modern texts, art, music and popular culture, and addresses the question of how we, in the late twentieth century, are to be competent and ethical readers of and responders to the "signs of the times."

Apocalyptic Bodies: the Biblical End of the World in Text and Image presents a cultural critical reading of apocalyptic texts and images, using a variety of critical perspectives, including body criticism, ideological criticism, and horror and fantasy theory. This innovative and provocative volume, which contains a selection of unusual apocalyptic images from folk art to old masters, offers new ways of thinking about the Bible and about the end of the world.

Tina Pippin is Associate Professor of Religious Studies at Agnes Scott College, Decatur. She is the author of *Death and Desire: the Rhetoric of Gender in the Apocalypse of John.*

APOCALYPTIC BODIES

The Biblical End of the World in Text and Image

Tina Pippin

London and New York

First published 1999
by Routledge
11 New Fetter Lane, London EC4P 4EE

Simultaneously published in the USA and Canada
by Routledge
29 West 35th Street, New York, NY 10001

Routledge is an imprint of the Taylor & Francis Group

Typeset in Garamond by Routledge
Printed and bound in Great Britain by Biddles Ltd, Guildford and
King's Lynn

British Library Cataloguing in Publication Data
A catalogue record for this book is available from the British Library

Library of Congress Cataloging in Publication Data
A catalogue record for this book has been requested

ISBN 0–415–18248–4 (hbk)
ISBN 0–415–18249–2 (pbk)

CONTENTS

ILLUSTRATIONS

PREQUEL, OR PREFACE

What are your favorite scary parts of the Bible? Do you try not to think about them, to avoid them, or look to the more pleasant parts of the Bible? One of my arguments in this book is that "apocalypse" is in excess in the Bible and in Western culture; apocalypse is not relegated to a fenced-in area in certain prophetic texts or gospels or the back of the Book. I explore several scenes of apocalypse in this book, scattered throughout the Hebrew Bible and the New Testament. By "apocalypse" I want to employ a broader definition that is about the end of the world but also any total destruction, or any revelation about "any catastrophe of such a scale that it seems to put this world in jeopardy" (Collins 1997: 1). My choices are a few among many, since there is much death and destruction in the Bible. I am also committed to a feminist reading that remembers and reveals the destruction of the human body, particularly women's bodies. The scary parts of the Bible I seek out in this study involve body parts. As in the film *Blue Velvet*, I have found a human ear on the ground, and it leads me into a world of horror.[1] "Let anyone who has an ear listen to what the Spirit is saying to the churches" (Apoc. 2: 11).

The Apocalypse of John (aka the Book of Revelation) provides the biggest crunch at the end of the Christian Bible, and I spend the most time in this book gazing at its horrors. I am fidgety in the Apocalypse of John; I think it opens forward and backward and sideways and all ways into other spaces. The excess is evident in the final "s" that so many people, including some biblical scholars, put on the end of the name of the last book, Revelation*s*. I imagine some of the academics are being cynical in their renaming of this narrative. Nonetheless, the Book of Revelation*s* is a created object, texts outside the text, excessive reading and writing. The Revelation*s* are legion and can only be tamed and regulated by dismissal, by over-reading, or by excessive fascination with the text and with the coming disasters.

One of my students recently said with a really worried look on her face, "I won't go into Revelation by myself." The Apocalypse and the apocalyptic are most safely read from a safe distance, and traditional historical-critical methodologies offer the best defenses against the horrors of the text. Part of my motivation to produce one more book on the apocalyptic and add it to the millennial craze at the end of the century is my dissatisfaction with only asking the questions about authorship, date, social world, and the like. Or maybe adding one more book only adds to the apocalyptic horror, to the traces of dead trees which are surely signs of the end of time.

I imagine that the debates about the inclusion of some of the apocalyptic parts of the Bible in some way share similarities with contemporary mixed feelings about the horror genre. The Apocalypse of John certainly had a difficult time in the canonical voting, but the alternatives were bloodier tours of hell. The main support came from the church leaders in Rome, and I learned in seventh-grade Latin class how the Romans engaged in debaucheries that led to their fall. I am using the cynicism of this false reading of history to show how such attitudes about apocalypse may have developed. Apocalypse is a blob in/on the New Testament; it is not confined to the last book of the Bible. As in that classic horror movie, *The Blob*, apocalypse grows as it eats up more textual space. At the turn of the twentieth century apocalypseblob has almost completely taken over Christian evangelical television. Prophecy shows read for The End in every corner of the news. There is great ecstasy in describing the end time horrors. Still, only certain religious sensibilities indulge in these texts.

I also want to rethink what a gender reading of the Apocalypse means, since more and more I am discovering that the categories are ambiguous and complex. A non-literal reading creates distance so that gender remains symbolic, not physical, and the gender-specific violence is tamed. A more literal reading which takes seriously the gendered images of Whore, Lamb, God, Beasts, and 144,000 could be seen as "low class"; literalistic readings should be left to the Christian fundamentalists. I choose to take the violence at face value and condemn it, but obviously in a different way than Christian fundamentalists. Many scholars (Yarbro Collins, Thompson, Barr, Schüssler Fiorenza) argue that the violence is acceptable since it is against the colonizing power, Rome. As a citizen of a colonizing power, I find that "Rome" is essentialized by these readings. The

Roman government and military may be evil, but no one speaks of the Roman people. Fundamentalist prophecy reports essentialize "Iraq" as the evil power, and try unsuccessfully to fit Saddam Hussein into the role of Anti-Christ. There is no democracy in the Apocalypse; God is as much a power of domination as any other power, only this apocalyptic manifesto calls for total obedience.

> But the throne of God and of the Lamb will be in it, and his servants will worship him; they will see his face, and his name will be on their foreheads. And there will be no more night; they need no light of lamp or sun, for the Lord God will be their light, and they will reign forever and ever.
>
> (Apoc. 22: 4–5)[2]

Does not a liberatory reading call on readers to resist the powers of domination in the struggle for democracy?

What am *I* doing here, once again, immersing myself in the discourse of disaster? As I speak of the perversities of apocalypse, am I not also drawn in by the evil? The image that comes to mind is of a common theme in movies where a good detective sets out to stop the evil, usually psycho, killer and is sucked into the vortex of the terror, suddenly unstable on her or his moral high ground.[3] I am fascinated by the cultural phenomenon of biblical apocalypse, by the destruction announced by Jesus, by the scattering at the Tower of Babel, by the body parts left at the death scene of Jezebel, and by the report of the character John of the Whore of Babylon and the Bride of Christ and the Last Judgment. I am a detective looking for clues at the crime scene – for body parts, heaps of bodies, the DNA of deities. And like the FBI agents in *The X-Files* I encounter the paranormal, the supernatural in my search. Many parts of my discoveries are inexplicable, mysterious. In every reading I do of the biblical apocalyptic I desire a more stable text; every new reading disrupts the previous reading, and on and on. My previous reading always seems naive and incomplete. How does one gain a balance between finding and facing the apocalyptic horror without giving in to it?[4] I believe all biblical scholarship gives in to the sublime horror of apocalypse to some extent. I give in because as I am committed to hunt down and expose the ethical problems of these texts, I am also drawn in by the textual power – the scenes of violence and death. I experience a double inclination to reject biblical apocalypse and its inherently disturbing deities and also to enter into its depths, like Alice in *Through the Looking Glass*. Is it possible to retain an ethical critique in the midst of such pleasurable reading? Is my dilemma itself a source of pleasure? Is this pleasure excessive?

Jack Zipes offers a recent revision of traditional views on fantastic literature. He differs from Tzvetan Todorov and Rosemary Jackson who believed that the fantastic causes the reader to hesitate by positing that Bible fantasy does not cause more anxiety, but it provides a place for "spiritual regeneration" (1998: xi) and "the resisting force of hope" (1998: xii). I agree with Zipes that Bible fantasy provides hope in the midst of world anxiety, but I want also to add that the biblical apocalyptic fantasy heightens the uncanny, the awe, and anxiety as the readers encounter the destructive deity. This horror may give believers hope that the utopian afterlife will make the earthly horrors worthwhile, but the complete trust given the supreme powers is full of cracks. Apocalypse is an uncertain certainty, a dreaded hope, an endless end. Apocalypse scares and scars; there are scars on the land (e.g. Babel, the old earth passing away) and on the human body (e.g. Jezebel's head, the absent space in the field, the mark on the forehead). Is there a time before the scar(e)s? A prequel to the events of terror?

This preface is a prequel because it represents my curiosities before I enter into the apocalyptic landscapes. The ideas in this volume were heard by the ears of many people who had a part in this prequel. I give special gratitude to my cohort in the research of the biblical fantastic, George Aichele, for a steady sense of theories and an openness to the unusual. He offered important suggestions on most parts of this book. J. Michael Clark and Bob McNeir endured frequent "apocalyptic updates" and gave me space to ask wild questions. Elizabeth Castelli offered an insightful response to the Mark 13 material at the 1994 Society of Biblical Literature annual meeting in Philadelphia. Jan Tarlin helped me sort out the tangled ideas in the concluding sections. Members of the Bible and Culture Collective heard the early renditions of the Babel material and offered support: George Aichele, Fred Burnett, Elizabeth Castelli, Tamara Eskanazi, Danna Nolan Fewell, David Jobling, Gary Phillips, and Ronald Schleifer. I am also grateful to Elisabeth Schüssler Fiorenza and David Barr for their on-going critiques of my first book and the conversations that continue to provide motivation for me to push further in my readings. My colleague in the Department of Religious Studies, John Carey, listened patiently and supportively to the newer ideas. Many of my colleagues at Agnes Scott College heard and saw the first run of the apocalyptic fear material and offered contagious humor and energy. Also, the students in my Fall 1997 "Apocalypse and Revolution" course inspired me with our creative "Apocalypse Watch" (see Magner 1997) and other projects that sought to uncover apocalypse in lived experience. Most of all, I want to thank my life partner, Jerry Gentry, for his open-heartedness and support in these apocalyptic times.

ACKNOWLEDGMENTS

Permission to use Chapters 2 and 3 is granted by Scholars Press. Chapter 2 appeared in a slightly different form in Janice Capel Anderson and Jeffrey L. Staley (eds) "Taking It Personally: Autobiographical Biblical Criticism," *Semeia* 72 (1995); Chapter 3 is a revised version of an article that appeared in George Aichele and Gary A. Phillips (eds) "Intertextuality and the Bible," *Semeia* 69/70 (1995).

Sheffield Academic Press granted permission to use Chapter 5: it is a revised version of an article in Elizabeth Struthers Malbon and Edgar V. McNight (eds) *The New Literary Criticism and the New Testament*, Journal for the Study of the New Testament, supplement, series 109, Sheffield: Sheffield Academic Press, 1994.

A different version of Chapter 6 appeared in George Aichele and Tina Pippin (eds) *Journal of the Fantastic Arts* 8/2 (1997).

Note: the publishers have made every effort to contact the authors/ copyright holders of works cited or reproduced in *Apocalyptic Bodies*. This has not been possible in every case, however, and we would welcome correspondence from those individuals/companies we have been unable to trace.

1

INTRODUCTION:
APOCALYPSE AS SEQUEL

Every apocalypse is a sequel. A sequel is a work which follows another work and can be complete in itself and seen in relation to the former and also what follows it. The story becomes the never-ending story, in ever-evolving renditions. Perhaps as a reader of the apocalyptic I do not want the end or the ending to come. Once more this is Derrida's apocalypse without apocalypse. This book is a sequel to my first book (Pippin 1992), which was a sequel to my dissertation, which was a sequel to my childhood in the apocalyptic South (see chapter 2), and so forth. The act of reading is a sequel to every previous reading.

What is God's sequel to the apocalypse? What is the oldest biblical apocalypse – the Jahwist version of the flood in Genesis, Isaiah's apocalyptic sections in Chapters 24–7, Ezekiel, Daniel? When was the first apocalyptic story told? It is impossible to know the origin, and the chaos of apocalypse cannot be essentialized. Perhaps apocalypse began at creation, out of the violence of creative chaos, and every retelling is a sequel, a trace of a trace of the journey toward the end of time.

The word "sequel" in its root is related to the words seal and sign. In apocalyptic literature the wise and prophetic words are sealed by the divine powers (Daniel 12: 9). In the Apocalypse of John the scroll of some of the visions has seven seals (5: 1–2), and only Lion/Root/Lamb is worthy to open the seals. The 144,000 are also sealed on their foreheads in order to escape the violence (Apoc. 7: 3, 4). The apocalyptic seal is protective. Seals hold back violence, but when opened unleash extreme violence, "the great day of wrath" (Apoc. 6: 17). Each of the seven seals harbors part of the destructive part of the scroll (cf. Apocalypse of Paul 41; Reddish 1990: 314). In the end John is told by the angel not to seal: "Do not seal up the words of the prophecy of this book, for the time is near" (22: 10).

1

The time is near, but the text spins around and around in constant re-readings and interpretive gestures. Billboards, evangelistic preaching, music, films, art – all these representations of the apocalyptic text in our culture break the seal on the biblical book(s). The seal on the forehead is a plague in the land. The 144,000 (in which groups like the Jehovah's Witness – with over six times that number in the United States – claim to have membership), becomes a leaky category; fake seals are popping out all over. The seal (of approval ...) will not hold, and besides, how can one tell an "authentic" seal? The seal is not a sign of safety as much as it is a sign of horror. A re-reading/replaying of the Apocalypse means a cycle of sealing, cracking open, and resealing, over and over again. The horror is replayed, reviewed, and the seal, like a closed door emanating strange noises, draws the victim toward it.

In contemporary horror films the sequel (and also the remake) is common. Wes Craven's recent sequel, *Scream 2*, self-consciously exposes the rules of the sequel; the character Randy, who in *Scream* pronounces the rules of the horror film, proclaims, "There are certain rules that one must abide by in order to make a successful sequel." In sequels the body count is always higher and there is more gore and more elaborate torture and killings. The killer/s always return in sequels. The same killers appear in biblical apocalypses: warrior angels, Satan, God. In the horror sequel, who survives in the end is predetermined but never certain. In postmodern horror the protagonist female survives (e.g. the character Nancy in the *Nightmare on Elm Street* series; Sydney in the *Scream* pair). The plot twists may be different but certain rules apply, since there are survivors left on earth. Apocalyptic literature breaks the rules of sequels in some sense because nothing and no one survives on the earthly plane; the surviving "winners" may suffer martyrdom on earth but gain eternal life in heaven. The losers survive in a sense, so they can suffer eternal torture. The Apocalypse of John posits a new heaven and earth (21: 1), thus there is total destruction of the old. In biblical and extra-biblical apocalypses it is clear who wins and who loses; one only need believe in God in a certain way to be saved from the apocalyptic terrors. Even with this certainty, there is dis-ease, as exemplified in the film, *The Rapture*, where the central character panics at the end (the Rapture), refusing the grace of God and opting instead for hell. Performance artist Laurie Anderson (1995) also tells of this final panic in the story of her fundamentalist Christian grandmother's worry over whether or not to wear a hat as she prepared on her deathbed to meet Jesus. The certainty is never complete; there are cracks where the horrors of hell seep in and terrify the believer. Apocalypse is a more complete, comprehensive death, the extreme genocide. The destruction of everything is part of God's plan.

There is dis-ease at the end of a horror film as in a biblical apocalypse; one expects a sequel, a replaying of the violence in a grander scale. One inside joke in *Scream* is that sequels are never as good as the first film (a reference to Wes Craven's direction of the first *Nightmare*). The extra-biblical apocalypses, especially the early Christian ones, get bloodier and more detailed. How could an apocalypse get more extreme when it is already the extreme? What could be more violent than, in an example of an earlier apocalyptic prophecy, "Now the Lord is about to lay waste the earth and make it desolate, and he will twist its surface and scatter its inhabitants" (Isaiah 24: 1)? The assumption in apocalyptic literature is that there will be no one to repopulate the earth, not even an alcoholic father and his dysfunctional, incestuous family, as in the Genesis flood narrative.

The Apocalypse of John is a sequel of the Hebrew Bible and Pseudepigrapha; its details of the end time violence are more extreme. Sequels only produce more horror. Much of the Apocalypse of John (like Mark 13) comes from Daniel and other Hebrew Bible apocalypses. New Testament apocalypses are thus sequels of sequels. Some of the apocalypses in early Christianity (sequels of the earlier apocalypses) are even more descriptive than the Apocalypse of John. The best examples of these "tours of hell" are the Apocalypse of Peter (a canonical runner-up) and the Apocalypse of Paul (and much later Dante's *Inferno*). Fire torture is the most popular choice of God and the angels; sinners will burn with their idols (Apocalypse of Peter 5–6; Reddish 1990: 248–9). There is also a pit of fire filled with excrement and the most terrible things imaginable. In the Apocalypse of Peter women who commit infanticide or abortion suffer the taunts of their children "and the milk of the mothers flows from their breasts and congeals and smells foul, and from it come forth beasts that devour flesh, which turn and torture them for ever with their husbands..." (Ch. 9; Reddish 1990: 250–1). Worms eat out human intestines, angels use hot irons to burn flesh and eyes and to cut off the lips of deceivers (Ch. 9), and hang sinners up so that "flesh-eating birds" can tear the flesh (Ch. 10; Reddish 1990: 250–1). There are "wheels of fire, and men and women hung thereon by the power of their whirling" (Ch. 12; Reddish 1990: 252). In the Apocalypse of Paul the punishments increase as the

3

story goes on, so that by the end (Ch. 51) the angel guide has to say, "Whoever scoffs at the words of this apocalypse, I will punish him" (Reddish 1990: 324). In one scene a minister who failed in his job suffers tortures in a river of fire; angels strangle him with "an iron instrument with three prongs with which they pierced the intestines of the old man" (Reddish 1990: 311). When Paul weeps at the torturous horrors, the angel instructs him, "Are you weeping, when you have not yet seen the greater punishments?" (Reddish 1990: 314). The worst horrors include the fiery masses burning in the pit of hell while others suffer from extreme, eternal cold.

In both these apocalypses, as in the Apocalypse of John, there is the tease of heaven, the place of salvation. But far more space is given to evil and the vengeful, eternal attack on sinners; the catalog of sin/sinners and the fantasy of their destruction is much more interesting than the peaceful heavenly garden. Heaven is almost an afterthought in some of these apocalypses. Or at least the heavenly realm is the frame for the main action – earthly destruction and/or sufferings in hell.

The Bible does not allow the reader to stay in paradise for long. By the second chapter of Genesis the really interesting characters appear (the snake and Eve). Churches invest in performances of "tribulation trails," not in "heavenly comforts tours." The rash of apocalyptic films at the end of this century is another example of this rush to imagine the end – or the rush that imagining the end provides. Comets, asteroids, plagues of viruses, alien invasion, internal global war, and evil transmitted by fallen angels are all ways to imagine the worst sufferings. Some contemporary apocalyptic visions even add government conspiracies (*The X-Files*): "Trust no one. The truth is out there." One film, *Fallen*, has as its advertising logo the phrase, "Don't Trust a Soul." This film further advertises itself as a "supernatural thriller" in order to distance itself from the horror genre. The assumption in this film is that anything that falls out of heaven (or paradise or Eden) is evil (cf. *The Prophecy*). *The X-Files* also touts itself as a thriller, although many of the episodes are gorefests. Its evil appears to fall out of the sky, too; alien beings in cahoots with the US government who invade human bodies (especially the bodies of women: Mulder's sister, Scully, the women used as reproductive machines). The title of *The X-Files'* feature-length film is instructive: *Fight the Future*. While many of these popular apocalypses mock themselves, they tap into the "unthinkable" horror that must be thought about to keep it at a respectful distance.

In biblical literature there is a conspiracy in heaven, especially in the Book of Job, where God and Satan conspire against the man Job. To what ends will such conspiring go? The depths of human sin and God's eternal wrath are placed alongside human worth and God's eternal love. But revenge is more interesting than grace; the twisting apart of the earth is more interesting than the re-creation of paradise.

In his study of the psychology of Christian fundamentalist "endism," Charles Strozier defines the apocalyptic: "One might say, following Revelation, that the apocalyptic connotes the violent, the redemptive, the vengeful, and the hopeful ... also the predictive ... the terrible ... the grandiose ... and the climactic" (1994: 154). Blood hymns in some conservative Christian church traditions speak to these different aspects of the apocalyptic. The apocalyptic is the low-brow literature of the bible. It has only become popular with the "high-brow" set (e.g. Stephen Gould) with the approach of the millennium.

There is a strange need in the apocalyptic for the violence to be "over the top." Could an argument be made that such violent litera- ture leads to violent behavior? The "movies made me do it" defense is spoofed in *Scream 2*. For Mimi Rogers' character in *The Rapture*, her excuse for killing her daughter was basically, "The apocalypse made me do it." Christian militia groups, and millennial religious groups such as Jim Jones's group at Jonestown and Heaven's Gate, seem to be arguing the same defense.

Why is there the need for apocalpytic sequels, especially around the millennium? One immediate response could be: what kind of sick mind writes this stuff? Is the horror genre the artistic manifes- tation of a sick mind? Or are horror sequels political and psychological ways of revealing evil in our society? Have these apoc- alyptic sequels gone on too long? Does this genre represent a virus in the theological body? Or are these narratives necessary to clear the space for hope?

Re-(w)ri(gh)ting apocalypse

In a radio interview given during the siege of his compound in Waco, David Koresh proclaimed that "theology really is life and death" (Tabor and Gallagher 1995: 99). To a theologian, too, a theological interpretation of the Apocalypse is life and death. As a theologian Keller must opt for taking the text seriously in terms of competing with fundamentalist interpretations and "on behalf of sustainable and shared life in the present" (1996: 16). There is ever a desire for hope. The theme of hope keeps this text theologially viable.

Keller's important book on the end of the world is a cosmic reading of biblical texts; in other words, she is engaged with the very nature of the apocalyptic, with the disclosure, the revealing revelation that takes place in the texts. Is "The End" (1996: 2) an opening? Keller wants to re-open the Apocalypse, but it is not really necessary to re-open the Apocalypse; it was never closed. The Apocalypse is an open text. It opens up into our present. I agree that "we are *in* apocalypse" (1996: 12). Keller calls for "a scripturally grounded narrative engagement" (1996: 25), and this call and placement of apocalypse is a vital point for theological hermeneutics and ethics.

Keller then attempts to unravel that apocalyptic thread in Christian history by taking the reader on a whirlwind tour of apocalypse in Christian history. This historical survey and commentary is valuable and puts the biblical vision/s in perspective. The best example of where this survey is the most powerful is in the chapter, "De/colon/izing Spaces," in which Keller discusses the apocalyptic effects of Columbus's (Colón) landing in the Caribbean. Keller's survey opens up the reader to creative new perspectives on the open-endedness of "The End," especially to some of the oppressed voices silenced by dominant patriarchal history.

Keller calls for a "counter-apocalypse" that has a "drive for justice" (1996: 20). A counter-apocalypse affirms the realm of God as a realm of justice. Keller opposes Lee Quinby's "anti-apocalypse." Quinby defines anti-apocalypse in terms of feminism, which she sees as:

> implicated in apocalyptic desires for the end of (masculinist) time and the transcendence of (masculinist) space, including the space of the innately gendered body. Feminism can be, however, (and often is these days) *anti*-apocalyptic insofar as it is anti-essentialist, anti-universalist, and anti-eschatological.
>
> (1994: 36)

An example of this type of feminism is found in the redrawing of cultural icons by the Guerrilla Girls; their approach to the apocalyptic (especially politics) is to undermine it.

Even Sallie McFague and Rosemary Radford Ruether's more immanent god, the world as God's body, while dealing with the problem of a transcendent, distant god, cannot "fix" the Apocalypse's desire for the end in which a transcendent God reigns solely and supremely. The "apocalips" (Keller's wonderful play on the word) (1996: 304ff.) speak glossolalia, fragments of a message of hope I cannot translate.

Keller is enmeshed in a postmodern apocalypse. Richard Dellamora describes it as "to be post- means to be *beyond* closure in the field of newly opened textual possibilities" (1995: xi). Her feminist vision is important because she speaks boldly and accurately about the postcolonial, gender, ethnic implications of the text.

Keller wants to rewrite the Apocalypse, or rather, re(w)ri(gh)te the narrative – rewriting it on her own terms and re-righting out of the clinches of fundamentalist interpreters. Violence, anti-Jewishness, misogyny, divine judgment, eternal punishment, the destruction of the earth – Keller rewrites the narrative so that the violence and exclusivity of apocalypse is transformed, so that the violent text is all right. Christianity is intact in both these readings, as it should be, given their social locations. Keller relates, "I imagine ourselves converging upon a moment of opportunity: as our species careens to the brink, it will see, it will hear, it will turn around in time..." (1996: 36). In a similar vein, Donna Haraway expresses this anxiety through her discussion of a painting by Lynn Rudolph entitled *Millennial Children*. In this painting small guardian angels flank two young girls who embrace in the midst of an environmental apocalypse. Haraway states, "These are the children whose witness calls the viewer to account for both the stories and the actualities of the millennium" (1997: 40). It is a nightmare vision, and the children offer hope for the future. While I hold such hope that humans will wake up and avoid self-destruction (or else I would not be involved in the peace movement), I do not think the Apocalypse desires this end. In my own state, Georgia, there is the manufacture of Trident submarines, the "White Trains," the School for the Americas, and Newt Gingrich, to name a few disaster images.

In James Morrow's vision of hell in his novel, <u>Only Begotten Daughter</u>, Jesus gives up heavenly glory to set up a soup kitchen in hell (serving a morphine soup to the damned to ease their suffering). In Morrow's version of the second coming, the messiah is female, and she follows the devil to hell, where she meets her half-brother. Jesus says to his half-sister Julie Katz, during one of their lengthy theological debates, "I mean, how can you bring about utopia with one eye cocked on eternity?...Oh *now* I get it – that's how they accommodated my not returning, yes? They shifted the reunion to some netherworld" (1990: 186). Keller wants to shift the responsibility back to earth.

In returning back to earth, she also returns to the violence. In retelling the story of the apocalyptic as an open-ended narrative are we making God a serial killer? A god who returns with every reading to strike again? I desire the end, the end of the kind of salvation history into which the Apocalypse is luring us. Ultimately Keller (although other more conservative reviewers will certainly differ) is submitting to the authority of the biblical text. There is no end of a hegemonic historical-critical method that attempts to seal the biblical canon shut, even though the angel in Apocalypse 22: 10 says, "Do not seal up the words of the prophecy of this book, for the time is near." I can make no sense of the nonsense of such doomsday desire; the judgment of the Apocalypse is not hopeful, not redemptive for me. I want, with Derrida, an apocalypse *sans* apocalypse. As Derrida relates:

> an apocalypse without apocalypse, an apocalypse without vision, without truth, without revelation, *envois* (for the "Come" is plural in itself, in oneself), addresses without message and without destination, without sender or decidable addressee, without last judgment, without any other eschatology than the tone of the "*Viens*."
>
> (1993: 167)

Keller reminds us (based on Ernst Bloch's analysis) that hope is a moral action (1996: 122–5). But does the Apocalypse give us hope? In the Apocalypse hope comes through a rape, through massive violence and the total destruction of the earth. The believers revenge their victimness (martyrdom). So is there no hope? I would say no, but we look to the wrong texts and invest these texts with power. If hope is a moral action, we must be moral about the way we hope. Perhaps I despair over the biblical text; I do not choose to lay my hope there.

The Apocalypse sends a warning:

> I warn everyone who hears the words of the prophecy of this book: if anyone adds to them, God will add to that person the plagues described in this book; if anyone takes away from the words of the book of this prophecy, God will take away that person's share in the tree of life and in the holy city, which are described in this book.
>
> (Apoc. 22: 18–19)

Surely, we're all damned! Every interpreter – we are all adding to and subtracting from the book as we interpret it, as we write alternative midrashim on it, as we struggle with its hard message. Thus, I ask, why apocalypse? By this I mean why continue to conform to and make apocalyptic texts and theologies conform to peacemaking and liberatory sensibilities? Will playing with these texts and theologies transform the violent past? Why apocalypse? Keller has led me to play further with these apocalyptic images and ideas and to face the depths of my own past brushes with apocalypse, the apocalyptic fields of my childhood and the urban streets of my adulthood. Her book pushes us toward The Edge and gives the reader a vision of hope and direction for social change.

The ideology of apocalyptic fantasy

The women say that they perceive their bodies in their entirety. They say that they do not favour any of its parts on the grounds that it was formerly a forbidden object. They say that they do not want to become prisoners of their own ideology.

(Wittig 1971: 57)

...they cursed God for the plague of the hail, so fearful was that plague.

(Apoc. 16: 21)

Is the fantastic subversive or conservative literature? This question is hotly debated in fantasy studies. Another way of asking the question is to ask what value system/s the text upholds. Is ideology a spectre of Marx (Žižek; Derrida), the lived experience of material social life and eternal class struggle (Althusser)? With Rosemary Jackson (1981: 61) Žižek argues that fantasy is unconscious (1994b: 316). For Žižek, "ideological fantasy" is not a false illusion hiding the real but is "an (unconscious) fantasy structuring our social reality itself" (1994b: 316). Fantasy actually supports reality rather than masks it (1994b: 325–7). Ideological fantasy is a spectre that haunts because it raises unconscious desires. These desires can be subversive or not; ideological fantasy is often a tool of liberation or oppression in the readers' hands. For example, the Apocalypse of John has been used as a liberatory narrative (e.g. Pablo Richard) or an exclusionary text (e.g. prophecy shows on Trinity Broadcast

9

Network). I choose in my work to confront the violent, exclusionary history of the Apocalypse, name it as such, and show its influences and multiple retellings (sequels). In making this choice I am able to reveal only a few of the instances where the spectre appears. The spectre is still out there.

The search for unity in ideological fantasy lies in the realm of religion. Even though many secular apocalypses exists, I think the main fascination is with the supernatural involvement in evil. In the Bible wayward angels stray from heaven, competing for power and setting up their own realm of power. God crosses the boundary of heaven in human and spirit forms enacting random "justice." Humans search for wisdom and immortality, often figuring out the way to reach heaven, until God intervenes. Ideological fantasies of biblical apocalypse are forceful nightmares of the soul, engaging the rhetoric of warfare and ultimate ruin with the promise of hope and unity with the divine.

These outlines of ideological fantasy are based in Marx and Lacan. In her outline of fantasy, Jackson relies on the concepts of "the Real" (Lacan) and "the Unreal" (Christine Brooke-Rose). If, as Jackson believes, fantasy belongs in the realm outside the "real" and "outside the control of the 'word' and the 'look'" (1981: 179), then perhaps fantasy lies outside the control of The Word, that unifying concept of sacred scripture, divine pronouncement. All the neat, safe spaces where "the true meaning" of the text is supposed to be found are transgressed by fantasy. Stories of apocalypse transgress categories of "real" and "unreal" so that no attempt to control it through any interpretive means is fully successful. Perhaps the traditional search for absolutes of the historical-critical method is like a magic ring that endues its wearer with powers. This ring is ultimately destructive and must be destroyed, and it takes a brave adventurer (such as Frodo in *The Lord of the Rings* trilogy) to save (Middle) Earth by destroying the ring. In other words, I am not providing any magic ring for reading the biblical fantastic.

Jackson relates the transgressive nature of fantasy:

> Fantasies of deconstructed, demolished or divided identities
> and of disintegrated bodies, oppose traditional categories of
> unitary selves. They attempt to give graphic depictions of
> subjects *in process*, suggesting possibilities of innumerable
> other selves, of different histories, different bodies.
>
> (Jackson 1981: 177–8)

Or in Žižek's thought, "fantasies image the possibility of radical cultural transformation through attempting to dissolve or shatter the boundary lines between the imaginary and the symbolic. They refuse the latter's categories of the 'real' and its unities" (1997: 178). Apocalypse reveals what happens in the process of the de-creation, the end of time, where the human (and animal) body is targeted, as it was in Eden. The search for unity (and equality) with the deity ends up badly for characters in the Bible, particularly if they transgress the ideologies of the biblical God/s. Given the outcome of Eden and Babel and the Apocalypse, how can the human initiation of connection with the deity end with anything other than horror?

By fantasy Žižek basically means the psychoanalytical concept, not the literary genre; however, his investigation is insightful. He moves from concrete to abstract, against the grain of traditional *Ideologiekritik* (1997: 1). Žižek sets out to remove the "seven veils of fantasy," and one of his points is that "fantasy is the primordial form of *narrative*, which serves to occult some original deadlock" (1997: 10). Žižek sees a "plague of fantasies" in modern culture. For him fantasy is "objectively subjective" (1997: 119). In other words, things never seem as they appear, or appear as they seem. Fantasy provides several variations of the Other, so that a unified vision is impossible in the end. Žižek suggests that apocalytic fantasy is acted out in human history: through genocide. In a section entitled, "The Poetry of Ethnic Cleansing" (1997: 60ff.), Žižek shows how the genocide in the former Yugoslavia involved the ideological fantasy of danger and then a purified land. As in the Apocalypse, there is a poetry to cleansing. The poetry is gruesome, but it is full of desire nevertheless: "a fantasy constitutes our desire, provides its co-ordinates; that is, it literally 'teaches us how to desire'" (Žižek 1997: 7).

Thus, fantasy reveals the real horror of ideology (Žižek 1997: 6): "this nightmarish universe is not 'pure fantasy' but, on the contrary, *that which remains of reality after reality is deprived of its support in fantasy*" (1997: 66). Žižek describes this concept of horror best in his observation of how the Other is created: "The only way to experience the big Other in the Real is thus to experience it as the superego agency, the horrible obscene Thing" (1997: 81).[1] The Other is accused of stealing *jouissance* and is thus a representative of *jouissance* (1997: 32). In the Apocalypse this is best illustrated in the murder of the Whore. The desire is sexual, political, economic,

11

religious, and she must be destroyed. Žižek relates such scape-goating to the Nazi genocide of the Jews:

> The Horrible can also function as the screen itself, as the primordial void or antagonism. For example, is not the anti-Semitic demonic image of the Jew, the Jewish plot, such an evocation of the ultimate Horror which, precisely, is the phantasmic screen enabling us to avoid confrontation with the social antagonism?...This is the ultimate horror: not the proverbial ghost in the machine, but the machine in the ghost: there is *no* plotting agent behind it, the machine just runs by itself, as a blind contingent device.
>
> (1997: 40, note 5).

Žižek believes that ideology conceals "the underlying 'unbalanced,' 'uncanny' structure" (1997: 82). Ideology is a spectre haunting culture: "the 'sublime object of ideology' is the spectral object which has no positive ontological consistency, but merely fills in the gap of a certain constitutive impossibility" (1997: 76). The ghost in the apocalyptic machine is horrifically sublime.

There is a link between ideological fantasy and pornography in which "this excessive opening up" of revealing "easily reverts to an excremental repulsive intrusion" "one finds oneself in a slimy obscene domain" (1997: 68). Life is hell; shit happens; but there remains the impossible possibility, the excrement of the end times, of the Apocalypse of Paul's pit of hell, bodies spattered all over eternity.

2

A GOOD APOCALYPSE IS HARD TO FIND: CROSSING THE APOCALYPTIC BORDERS OF MARK 13[1]

Introduction

As a white, southern female growing up in the tobacco fields of eastern North Carolina, I was and am still able to observe and participate in the apocalyptic landscape of southern culture around the issues of race, class, gender/sexuality, and religion. The New Testament (especially the apocalyptic sections) was and is not so much a religious text as a cultural text for me. How do I write and teach authentically and responsibly about the New Testament as a cultural text in the context of the southern United States? The heavy exclusionary ideology of apocalyptic prophecy is similar to the contemporary ethos of racism, sexism, and classism, and other oppressive ideologies. Crossing the borders into Mark 13, the so-called "'little' apocalypse" (although apocalytic visions are never "little"!), I am entering into a world like the southern grotesque, where God's wrath and persecution by one's enemies is predominant. Flannery O'Connor and other southern writers express the theme of the southern apocalyptic in their fiction, and I want to draw on my own experiences and the literature and stories of the region in which I live and teach in order to tie these fictions together.

In this essay several theoretical voices converse with the experiential. Cultural studies in the postmodern apocalyptic, studies in fantasy (the supernatural) and horror theory, readings of southern fiction, and the ethical discourse about reading about the end of the world all form my reading of Mark 13. I read this narrative in terms of its "cultural presence" in my life and my students' lives. I push the boundaries of the traditional field of "Ethics of the New Testament" to show how a more intimate cultural reading offers an alternative to reconstructionist hermeneutics.

Signs of the times: autobiography and apocalypse

Many apocalyptic signs from my youth stick in my mind, but one predominates – a huge billboard in Smithfield, North Carolina, where my great uncle lived:

> Help Fight Communism & Intergration [sic]
> Join and Support United Klans of America Inc.
> KKKK Welcomes You to Smithfield.

This signifier had multiple, shifting signifieds; signs of white ignorance and privilege; signs of peace and war; signs of southern hospitality and deadly welcome. The traditional three-K abbreviation expands to four, the proliferation of the sign, endless horror.

Figure 2.1 Billboard on Highway 70 in Smithfield, North Carolina, 1960s–1970s

Source: Photo by the author.

Smithfield had signs like this one on the main road at either end of town, trapping the visitor or townsperson in a weird web of relationships anchored in deep and extreme racism. As a child looking up at these signs from the safety of my parents' car, I would imagine the strange hooded creatures around a burning cross shouting hate from the Bible. They were shrouded in myth and mystery for me, since I had never seen a Klansman and only knew of the stories of veiled horror. Early in my life I was a reader of apocalyptic texts; unavoidably so, as a southern female of white privilege in the upheavals of the 1960s. What was veiled then is slowly being revealed (re-veiled?) to me now: the existential apocalypse of oppression and injustice.

The Klan sign stayed up until the late 1970s. Recently, when I searched the county archives, there were embarrassed memories of the sign, but no recollection of any preserved photos or newspaper articles. Nor was there a file on the Klan, but in a file labeled "Human Relations," I found the only preserved document, a 1977 article from the Raleigh paper about the controversy of the sign's existence. Also kept in this file was a strange cardboard sign that hung on the city swimming pool in the 1960s: "This is KKK country," painted in red letters. The signs are now gone, or are they? There is hardly a trace in history; there is only what Paul Jay calls "visual memory" that aids in the construction of self-identity (1994: 191).

In my visual memory the KKKK sign has become a metonym for the South, although physical representations of this sign were almost completely erased. Leigh Gilmore points out the difference between metonymy and metaphor in autobiography: "The real clings to metonymy; metaphor shakes off the real and transcends materiality....[i]t is autobiography's metonymies that seem to ground it in real life" (1994a: 68). The sign was buried deep in the county archives, yet its trace lingers in memory and in social relations.

The trace of this material signifier is fragmented into many signs, both material and in memory. As part of my *bio*, my life, this sign forms the trace of my own ontological grounding. The sign was and is both fantasy and magic, appearing and disappearing over the years. To uncover it as I am doing now is to let the secret out. But the secret will remain secret for some – the secret will be whispered and shouted and hidden all at once. This is a problem of the apocalyptic as well: the secret signs are supposedly uncovered and made visible. Yet all the reader has is a trace, an echo of the end time.

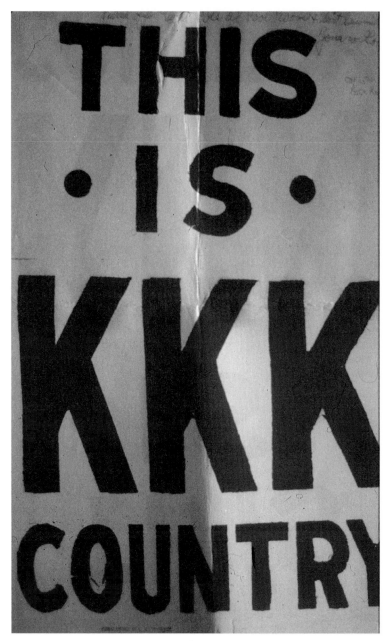

Figure 2.2 Sign on a public swimming pool in Smithfield, North Carolina, in the 1960s

Source: Photo by the author.

Antonio Gramsci wrote from prison that "the consciousness of what one really is [entails] 'knowing thyself' as the product of the historical process to date which has deposited in you an infinity of traces, without leaving an inventory" (1971: 324). Apocalypse, like the story of a life writ large, is an infinity of traces, of infinite horror and joy, infinite salvation and damnation. Somewhere in the midst of these traces of apocalyptic terrain is my life, my self. How do I find a social location that I believe is crucial to my autobiography and to autobiographical reading but also to the reading of apocalyptic? How do I locate apocalypse in my life and in the gospel narrative?

The signification of the billboard is, for me, apocalyptic because of its multiple meanings of privilege, oppression, and violence. The apocalyptic discourse of this sign forms a piece of who "I" am; the sign is part of the visual memory of my story. But my "self" as a white, southern female is also a signifier. Thus, the "truth" of the sign is different for me than for my family and different for me now than in my childhood. Gilmore relates "that the technologies of autobiography are conflictual through and through, derived as they are in relation to discourses of identity and truth which are themselves held together by means of some rhetorical violence" (1994a: 45). In the act of digging up the sign and making it visible again in order to deal with its metonymic violence, I am in Mab Segrest's terms a "race traitor." For I wish to re-trace, rather than reinscribe, my white privilege.

I lived in many worlds as a child: a factory town, tobacco fields in the summer, and private school. Now I teach at a private women's college in the South, where the hushed voices of the southern aristocratic women lull/dull my senses and seem to whisper subliminal messages: surface is everything; look good to the neighbors; cover up the embarrassing family secrets; avoid conflict at all costs; always be cordial; smile sweetly; end sentences in a question. One term for this institutional cover-up action is "anesthetized apartheid" (Gilbert Bond, personal communication). Apocalyptic signs wake me out of my southern stupor, shouting, "This is for real!" Racism is no fiction; no mythic past of Scarlett and Rhett at Tara. Adela Yarbro Collins (1984) is correct when she says apocalyptic literature is the literature of crisis and catharsis, but the crises and catharses have multiple focalizers.

It is difficult to locate the Markan apocalypse in a particular historical moment. The slippage of apocalypse into the cracks of history makes this view of the end a passing glimpse in Mark – in the parable in Chapter 4, in the Son of Man sayings, and in time markers such as 9: 1: "I tell you, there are some standing here who will not taste death until they see that the kingdom of God has come with power." This certain statement is untrustworthy. Are we also to believe Jesus when he says, "Be alert; I have already told you everything" (13: 23)?

Mark 13, the "'little' apocalypse," also deconstructs itself: "But about that day or hour no one knows, neither the angels in heaven, nor the Son, but only the Father. Beware, keep alert; for you do not know when the time will come" (Mark 13: 32–3). This Markan passage deconstructs like the passage at the end of the Apocalypse of John (22: 10–11): "Do not seal up the words of the prophecy of this book, for the time is near. Let the evildoer still do evil, and the filthy still be filthy, and the righteous still do right, and the holy still be holy." The reader is taken to the edge and then snatched back. The time is near but not yet. Elizabeth Struthers Malbon concludes, "Mark 13 deconstructs itself as an anti-apocalyptic eschatological discourse. It moves not from no knowledge to uncovered knowledge, but from presumed knowledge to no knowledge" (1995: 26). I agree with her last sentence, but not her first. The question of the disciples, "Tell us, when will this be...?" ultimately remains unanswered. The implied reader is told, "Truly I tell you, this generation will not pass away until all these things have taken place" (Mark 13: 29), but there is again an unstable timetable between the disciples, the implied reader, and any other readers, textual and extratextual. Jesus is telling the mystery and at the end of the apocalyptic narrative the mystery remains. Dan Via says that "revelation is both given and withheld" (1985: 57). Stephen Moore questions, "But does apocalypse, uncovering, yield *parousia*, or presence in Mark? The *parousia* of the thing sought can be glimpsed, but can it ever be grasped?" (1992: 32). In its deconstructive move Mark 13 rejects the reader at the end, spitting her out and back into the story of the passion of Jesus. The presence or coming of the end cannot be grasped, but it can enter under our skin and into our subconscious, putting us on edge: border-crossing into the horrors of the end. The apocalypse in Mark 13 slips in between Jesus' ministry and passion, into the cracks of history and the abyss of imagination.

As there are vague details of the coming horrors to serve as markers, the time is also uncertain. This uncertainty of when the Apocalypse will occur leaves the reader fearful, for God is going to come suddenly (Mark 13: 36). Awake or asleep, the horrors are massive, but there are no certain and clear historical markers to prepare the reader adequately. The horror will sneak up and grab you from behind, if you are not looking (and maybe if you are). Apocalypse is the eye/I of the storm (God's storm/God's story), just as autobiography is the "I" of the storm. Apocalypse is the ultimate erasure of the I of humanity and the end of the human story.

Just as it is difficult to locate apocalyptic literature in history, so also is it difficult to locate autobiography in history. Autobiography as a mode has had a mixed reputation. As Paul de Man states, "autobiography always looks slightly disreputable and self-indulgent" (1979: 919). If apocalyptic literature is resistance literature (Barbara Harlow's term, 1987), then this resistance is multiple. My own resistance to my cultural heritage and my (dominant) culture's resistance to me and my cultural identity are continued crises. Apocalypse creates an anxiety, like living in the South; what is under the surface always rises. The sign exists, even if there were no text or image, but only memory.

Autobiographical literary theory puts up front the notion that the acts of reading and interpreting are subjective. But it does more than this; the interpreter has to be intentionally conscious and confessional. Autobiographical literary criticism admits to the "stuff" of reading: the fallacies, the commitments, and the cultural markers. Traditional New Testament studies, the kind still dominant in introductory textbooks, admit to nothing but a series of "objective truths," without acknowledging the phallacies of Enlightenment, overwhelmingly white, heterosexual, first-world, male power readings. Can a genre have a race, a sexuality, and an endless series of other markers? Autobiography admits to gender – and more and less – depending on the teller.

Is the Markan Apocalypse a hospitable place to visit, autobiographically, as the narrator jerks us "immediately" from scene to scene? What signs do we see? "Help fight insurrection and cultural intergration [sic]: the colonial power of Rome welcomes you to Palestine." Or as a sign on entering Mark 13: "Help fight temple authoritarianism and false messiahs: the apocalyptic God welcomes you to the end of time. Watch your step – and your back." The apocalypse promises and threatens violence, and it does so in cosmic terms. How can the autobiographical be an ethical (re)source? How can apocalyptic be an ethical (re)source?

Ethics in/of the New Testament: getting a word in edgeways

Apocalyptic discourses and literature have often been embarrassments for New Testament scholars, like some bad relative with a prison record. After all, what is Jesus, the preacher of love and inclusivity, doing telling and enacting horror stories of the end time? Moore's deconstructive reading of Mark is instructive:

> Bar(r)ed a(cce)ss – Mark bares only to bar, embarrassing his interpreters.
> This book of reveilation reviles all who would arrest it....What if its reveilation were misunderstood, mutilated by the exegete, its left *i* poked out by the exegete's pen in an attempt to read it as revelation?
>
> (1992: 32)

Yet most New Testament exegetes read Mark 13 as revelation – either by toning down the apocalyptic tone into a broader eschatological discourse or by seeing the chapter as a call to ethical action encouraged by an imminent end of time. Some evangelical scholars even revel in the revelation. In marked contrast, the Jesus Seminar designates in black (does black then equal inauthentic, and is their reading a white supremist one?!) most of Mark 13, except for a few gray areas: the statement about the destruction of the temple (13: 2); a brief saying about the false messiahs (13: 21); part of the fig tree story (13: 28–9); the uncertainty of the time (13: 32); and part of the landlord image (13: 34–6) (Funk et al. 1993: 108–14). Thus, this group of scholars believes that the heavy apocalyptic discourse is not authentic to Jesus. Their retelling of the Apocalypse is of a marginal apocalypse, only mildly offensive.

Mark 13 is a narrative in the middle of a biography (a gospel) in which Jesus tells of both the destruction of the world and his own role in the end. Malbon sees Mark 13 as part of the narrative whole of Mark, paralleling the passion in Mark 14–16. She connects the command "to watch" with the verb "raised," which she calls "double endings," "and both endings are open-ended" (1995: 15). Likewise, Robert Fowler focuses on the narrative function of this chapter by examining "the function of Mark 13 as the discourse of the narrator" (1991: 87). What is important is what is going on at the level of narrative (the narrator and extranarrative audience: implied reader and narratee).

In terms of the narrative space in Mark 13, as in the Apocalypse of John, the imagery is vivid. There are wars, the destruction of the temple, earthquakes, famines, birthpangs, beatings, trials, betrayals, murders, hatred, salvation, suffering, the darkening of the sun and moon, and falling stars. Mark 13 is an outline of the events expanded upon in the Apocalypse of John; yet even this quick tour of apocalypse is effective and deadly.

For ethicists there is either disdain for the apocalyptic in the New Testament, especially when it appears in the gospels, or much hard work undertaken to make the apocalyptic fit into a just new order. Even those who admit to apocalyptic material in the gospels, like ethicist Allen Verhey, do not want to connect Jesus to this mode of discourse: "to reduce Jesus to an apocalyptic seer is also a misunderstanding for he breaks through the forms and categories and pessimistic determinism of apocalyptic" (1984: 15). But in Mark, the real Messiah will be known by these apocalyptic signs, and the reader is warned to beware of false messiahs. "Many will come in my name and say, 'I am he!' and they will lead many astray" (Mark 13: 6). Dan Via wants to retain a "demythologized apocalyptic" from Mark in his New Testament ethics, and suggests that "this connection between apocalyptic and ethics should also be maintained by constructive Christian ethics" (1985: 7). Ethics and narrative are bound together, so that the act of reading leads to action. Via considers the teaching of Jesus to be about more than the eschatological kingdom of God; there is also the socio-historical, demythologized, apocalyptic narrative. How can the apocalyptic be demythologized, autobiographized? Isn't its very power in its presence and absence as myth?

Ched Myers' solution to the ethical dilemma of reading Mark 13 is to find an ethic of nonviolent resistance in this final, public speech of Jesus. Myers does a historically reconstructive reading and assigns a pre-70 CE date to the text. In light of the time of war he states, "Mark prepares the reader for a discourse not of revolutionary triumphalism, but of suffering and tribulation. Against rebel eschatology, Mark pits the death/life paradox of his own narrative symbolics and the politics of nonviolence" (1988: 333). Myers sees Mark as opposing the urban, temple-based, religious culture and also in opposition to the armed-insurrectionist option. Thus, Mark is debating the upper-class Jewish religious authorities and the rebel forces. The elect will patiently endure all the terrors, while keeping intent watch on the return of Jesus. "For Mark, it is the culmination of Jesus' sermon on revolutionary patience" (1988:

347–8). Myers has Jesus sounding like Gandhi in Mark 13. The ethical requirements of the elect to follow nonviolence are the opposite of the ethic of the violent deity.

In revisionist exegesis all of the parts of the New Testament must fit into an acceptable ethic of justice. One major problem is that the diversity of the New Testament becomes molded into one monolithic ethic. The New Testament becomes a whole piece, a seamless garment, a unified self. As "sacred text" this canon must meet certain ethical standards, and the uneven or questionable parts made marginal or smoothed back into the whole.

In Mark 13 there is a system of privilege in terms of the saved and the damned. To have the elect there must also exist the Others: outsiders, outcasts, the mirrored double, the evil twin, the pathetic victim. "For in those days there will be suffering, such as has not been from the beginning of the creation that God created until now, no, and never will be. And if the Lord had not cut short those days, no one would be saved..." (Mark 13: 19–20). Is this suffering to be worse than the Flood? Is the creator trying to get back to the "origin"? Here is God as monster once again, raining/reigning terror on creation; with Jesus, God threatens to roam the earth and stand outside the gates, breathing heavily: "Behold I stand at the door and knock" (Apoc. 3: 20). Could Mark 13 be a parody of the apocalyptic – do not trust anyone who comes with this grotesque message?

This imminent end of the world is a postmodern mosaic of horror with people fleeing for the hills. In the rhythm of Mark's gospel Chapter 13 is the ultimate doom before the doom of Jesus' death. Before the Crucifixion the reader knows there will be payback. The Son of Man will return with his heavenly hosts. Heavenly hospitality is not inclusive. Everything will pass away – except Jesus' words. "All things came into being through him, and without him not one thing came into being" (John 1: 3). All things come to an end through him. The "I" is disrupted and fractured; "I am he" (Mark 13: 6) is an impostor. Or is he? Is Jesus in Mark 13 the real impostor? In the beginning was the Word, and in the end is the Word, while the earth falls silent.

How is the self re/de/constructed at and during the end of the world? Apocalypse puts the reader on edge; when the self is on the edge, what happens to story? to autobiography? Are the voices thrown into the abyss? Does/must God always have the last word? Can I get a word in edgeways? I refuse to read the apocalyptic as an acceptable ethical narrative, but I'm not saying that apocalyptic literature is inferior in the New Testament. The apocalyptic discourse cannot simply be excised. Apocalypse permeates every narrative in Mark, leaking out of the mouths of narrators, characters, and deities. Similarly, as Gilmore points out, "The mark of autobiography is a discursive effect, an effect of reading in relation to certain discourses. Thus, the mark of autobiography creates an enlivening instability in both text and context" (1994b: 7). If God has the last word on earth, then who is there to hear?

What is the ethic of apocalypse, the sign of autobiography? Is this destruction in Mark 13 acceptable? Why do Christians operate under this ethic? It hovers and lingers in Christian texts, denials, and actions. Is the only way to paradise through a bloody coup, offering up heaps of bodies to a bloodthirsty god? What kind of covenant is "apocalypse"? Is this an amoral deity poised to run amok on the world? A creator on a destructive, destroyer's binge? Is it "legal" and ethical for the deity to destroy? Is God held to a different moral standard? Is Jesus off the hook because "only the Father" knows the hour of the disaster? What does it mean to read this text ethically? What are we watching for? Have we become co-conspirators with God, enabling global disasters and mass genocide?

A good apocalypse is hard to find

What do you immediately think of when you read the words "southern accent?" Once at a teaching workshop I was asked by someone from the northern United States if I forced my students to speak in my accent. The appropriate comeback would have been, "No, do you?" But the chill of the learned, moderate shame over my southern accent crept in even as I laughed at the joke, stifling any reply. In the library exhibit of Flannery O'Connor at Milledgeville College there is a videotape of a television interview with O'Connor in the 1950s. My immediate reaction upon hearing her speaking voice for the first time was of shock; she sounded just like my aunt from Georgia. The Iowa Writers' Workshop and years in Connecticut had not diminished O'Connor's heavy southern drawl. I wanted O'Connor to sound different, educated, but she spoke in an accent that exposed my biases about my own region. So I experienced a double shame: shame over my own origins and culture and shame over thinking that my heritage was inferior. Although as a child (and adult) I fought the strong regionalism dividing North and South and the South's continuing to fight the Civil War (replayed in terrible phrases like, "The South's gonna rise again"), I bought into the attitude that southern speech could not reflect intelligence.

Perhaps my shame and embarrassment over this piece of my autobiography is similar to my struggle with the presence of the apocalyptic in the New Testament. Is Mark 13 like that sign in Smithfield, a part of culture that good folks will not acknowledge? As a fiction writer, O'Connor is curious about the apocalyptic signs of southern culture. Although she is not without her own racist assumptions in her writing, she writes about the southern gothic and apocalyptic terrain in ways that expose its shame and its regional secrets. Today, whenever I leave the metropolitan center of Atlanta and visit other parts of Georgia (or the South), I feel as if I am in a different, earlier time. Likewise, I tend to date the educational institution where I teach at around 1952 in terms of its attitudes and "plantation mentality." This is the time of O'Connor's major writings, and 1952 is when she wrote "A Good Man Is Hard to Find," the story I want to use as paradigmatic for her apocalyptic vision. In O'Connor's stories I am on familiar ground. She exposes the manners and meanness of southern traditions.

In "A Good Man Is Hard to Find" a repressed son, Bailey, his mannered mother, and his wife and three children take a vacation trip to Florida from Atlanta. But when they take a dirt road to find an old house that the Grandmother reminisces about, a cat she had hidden in a basket in the back seat escapes, causing Bailey to wreck the car. Along comes a car full of escaped convicts led by the Misfit, and they murder the whole family, leaving the dead bodies in a pile in the woods.

This story is particularly violent. And its violent end is proleptically announced when the Grandmother calls attention to a newspaper article about the "Misfit" and his actions. "I wouldn't take my children in any direction with a criminal like that aloose in it. I couldn't answer to my conscience if I did," she says (1982: 117). On the way to Florida the Grandmother insists they search for the old plantation outside of Toomsboro (pun), and the car overturns on a dirt road. After the wreck the family sits in a ditch: "Behind the ditch they were sitting in there were more woods, tall and dark and deep" (1982: 125). "Behind them the line of woods gaped like a dark open mouth" (1982: 127). O'Connor reported on the writing of this story and its violence:

Violence is never an end in itself. It is the extreme situation that best reveals what we are essentially.... Violence is a force which can be used for good or evil, and among other things taken by it is the kingdom of heaven. But regardless of what can be taken by it, the man in the violent situation reveals those qualities least dispensable in his personality, those qualities which are all he will have to take into eternity with him.

(1969: 113–14)

The apocalyptic is "the extreme situation" and extreme violence. Apocalypse is the true test of character, for when the violence comes there is no chance to repent. In Mark the best preventive measure is staying awake and watching for the end.

In O'Connor's story the Misfit defines the terms for an ethic of the end: "I found out that crime don't matter. You can do one thing or you can do another, kill a man or take a tire off his car, because sooner or later you're going to forget what it was you done and just be punished for it" (1982: 130–1). Later he asks, "Does it seem right to you, lady, that one is punished a heap and another ain't punished at all?" (1982: 131). In an interchange between the Grandmother and the Misfit she invokes religion: "Finally she found herself saying, 'Jesus, Jesus,' meaning, Jesus will help you, but the way she was saying it, it sounded as if she might be cursing" (1982: 131). The Misfit finds problems with this Jesus: "'Jesus was the only One that ever raised the dead.' The Misfit continued, 'and He shouldn't have done it. He thrown everything off balance.... No pleasure but meanness'" (1982: 131). "'Maybe He didn't raise the dead,' the old lady mumbled..." (1982: 132).

The thin veil between faith and unbelief is the thin veil of ultimate loss and gain in apocalyptic fiction, like the thin line between lying and truth-telling in autobiography. Either way you go you encounter the violent wrath of God, which throws everything off balance and is "no pleasure but meanness." As V.S. Naipaul suggests about the South: "Religion was like something in the air, a store of emotion on which people could draw according to their need" (1982: 69).

In some concluding remarks the Misfit adds, "'She would have been a good woman,' the Misfit said, 'if it had been somebody there to shoot her every minute of her life'" (1982: 133). This threat of being shot every minute leads to the possibility of redemption for O'Connor. To be one of the elect one must come face to face with one's own limitations and sinful state. The threat of apocalypse any minute in Mark 13 leads to a decision to be part of the elect.

O'Connor scrapes off the manners and goes straight for the meanness of southern culture and human nature. She uses grotesque images and metaphors which are often familiar and comic in detail. For example, in the description of the Grandmother's dress she writes: "In case of an accident, anyone seeing her dead on the highway would know at once that she was a lady" (1982: 118). Ralph Wood comments that in O'Connor's fiction "the grotesque is the artistic means O'Connor employs for this necessary act of theological aggression" (1988: 112). This negative view of God's actions in the world is also the way the grotesque works in the apocalyptic; it is aggressive and horrifying. Edward Kessler notes the extreme violence of O'Connor's story and that it is not the murders "but the violence done to familiar ways of thinking; the good man is hard to find because he cannot be defined" (1986: 63). In apocalypse is a good God hard to find?

As an Episcopalian I thought I grew up biblically illiterate, especially concerning the apocalyptic. While the apocalyptic was and is marginally part of the "canon" of my church, I live in the midst of an apocalyptic culture. Autobiographical literary theory has made me think about why I chose to do research on apocalyptic literature for my dissertation. I was reading these "texts" all around me as a child of the South. Like the protagonist in David Lynch's film *Blue Velvet* (filmed in eastern North Carolina), I have found a human ear on the ground. When he chooses to pursue the mystery, the safe, small-town atmosphere flips, and the innocent world becomes an horrific underworld of crime and violence. O'Connor chose to pursue the mystery and enter into the violent, torturous plot of human relations using the form of the southern grotesque. Autobiographical criticism gives me tools to negotiate this territory and deal with the ethical implications and concerns that apocalyptic texts and cultures provoke. When I read O'Connor's fiction or the fiction of Mark 13, I am on a precarious edge between my "safe" world and the imagination of ultimate horror. The edge of apocalypse is the edge of the ethical, a possible journey into a destructive future. For O'Connor as for Mark, salvation is through violence.

Southern culture on the skids

I was standing over the potato salad at a Baptist Peace Fellowship of North America potluck when I first met Will Campbell. At the time he was a visiting professor in my home state at UNC Wilmington. When I told him where I was from, we immediately began trading, "I betchas": "I bet you've never heard of this small town in eastern North Carolina." He thought he had me on a tiny crossroads called Ormondsville, but I was able to name the tobacco farmer for whom I worked for over two summers in early high school. Then the revelation occurred: that this farmer was a Grand Wizard in the Ku Klux Klan, and that the region's elite private school I attended with his son was founded on racist principles.

What I had not realized when I read Campbell's memoir, *Brother to a Dragonfly* (1977), years before in college was that Campbell had chosen this Klansman to befriend. This Wizard was eventually kicked out of the Klan, but none the less this man and the fields and barns I worked in represent for me the apocalyptic text and geography of the South. As a female of white privilege who worked side-by-side with tenant farmers, a majority of whom were African American, I saw two worlds watching and listening to the effects of racism on people's lives. For me the tobacco field was what Gilmore calls "a site of identity production" (1994b: 4). I learned what happened at the end of each work day: I went home to a different place, an all-white neighborhood on the edge of a small, textile plant town. And at the end of each season I was able, because of my summer earnings, to attend an all-white private school. I had indoor plumbing and new shoes for school and books and opportunities, while my co-workers had small, two-room, wooden-frame houses and little way out of the cycle of poverty of seasonal minimum wage.

In the retelling of his own life story Campbell is moved to make revelatory connections. Because of his connections, I am able to connect my story with Campbell's, although we are from different generations. Both stories kick up the dust of memory and I am led to re-trace the apocalyptic terrain of race in my southern life. Paul de Man comments: "Writers *of* autobiographies as well as writers *on* autobiography are obsessed by the need to move from cognition to resolution and to action, from speculative to political and legal authority" (1979: 922). Campbell moves toward resolution by putting a face on the Other and by seeing in that face his own reflection. He decides to expose the Klansman's secret life:

"How about telling me what the Ku Klux Klan stands for?"

It was as if he had been waiting for me to ask.

"The Ku Klux Klan stands for peace, for harmony, and for freedom."

"Now one more question. What means are you willing to use to accomplish those glorious ends?"

"Oh. Now I see what you're getting at. The means we are willing to use are as follows: murder, torture, threats, blackmail, intimidation, burning, guerrilla warfare. Whatever it takes."

And then he stopped. And I stopped. I knew that I had set a trap for him and had cleverly let him snap the trigger.

But then he started again. "Now, Preacher. Let me ask you a question. You tell me what we stand for in Vietnam."

Suddenly I knew a lot of things I had not known before. I knew that I had been caught in my own trap. Suddenly I knew that we are a nation of Klansmen. I knew that as a nation we stood for peace, harmony and freedom in that war, that we defined the words, and that the means we were employing to accomplish those ends were identical with the ones he had listed.

(1977: 247–8)

The traditional line about the gospels is that they reveal a God of peace, harmony, and freedom. In the Gospel of Mark is there a God of peace or one of wrathful violence, or both? The apocalypse is to occur by mass murder and destruction; whatever it takes. Is Mark 13 and other apocalyptic literature like the Klan's and Campbell's revelation? If the root meaning of apocalypse is to reveal, to take the lid off, to uncover, could it not also mean "to take the hood off"? Is God wearing a hood in Mark 13? Is there a burning cross in Mark? A vision of the worst of human actions, the mass lynching of the Others, is what we project onto the deity. What happens in the Markan apocalypse – is the hood ripped off only to show yet another mystery? Fooling us again and again yet pounding us with the possibility of the horrors?

Why did I ever think this apocalypse was ethically acceptable? From the position of "privilege" as a Christian, I just never thought about the violence. Mary Ann Tolbert offers a blunt reminder, "We do not protest our privilege; we protest our pain" (1995a: 265). As I examine my culture, my life, I am now reading Mark 13 as a text of a violent God. Is the Misfit in O'Connor's story leading us through our repression of Jesus' involvement in the violence by revealing that with Jesus there is "no pleasure but meanness" (1982: 131)? The Misfit, like the Klansman, sees clearly how God is working. I am only now beginning to make the connections between the KKKK sign, southern fiction and the stories of mythic and divine violence, the Klansman, and the lingering veil of the biblical apocalyptic. Apocalyptic violence is on the surface – in the sign, in the tobacco fields, in the gospels, in Paul – not isolated in some not too distant future. Flannery O'Connor observes:

> By and large people in the South still conceive of humanity in theological terms. While the South is hardly Christ-centered, it is most certainly Christ-haunted. The Southerner who isn't convinced of it is very much afraid that he may have been formed in the image and likeness of God.
>
> (quoted in Ketchin 1994: xi)

The apocalyptic order in Mark 13 reveals what has been going on all along in southern culture and can no longer be repressed and denied. Apocalyptic literature reveals to me the violence of the South of my childhood and the "'New' South" in which I live today. The Markan violence reveals how "Christ-haunted" my life in the South has been and is now. "And if anyone says to you at that time, 'Look! Here is the Messiah!' or 'Look! There he is!' – do not believe it" (Mark 13: 21). Where is the true Messiah of the Markan apocalypse? Is the apocalypse telling me I am made in "the image and likeness of God," and if so, which Messiah do I choose? According to Mark 13, I am either saved or damned, and if saved, I am to be responsible, "awake," in the midst of the violence, patiently enduring the end time suffering. Paradise awaits those who follow these teachings. Mark 13, like the apocalyptic signs of my region, is visible at the entrance of paradise. Peace, harmony, and freedom. I feel trapped by this vision of violence. So I dig in the archives of biblical exegesis on the Markan apocalypse and the archives of my life. And as I reject and leave this vision of paradise, I glimpse yet another apocalyptic sign.

Figure 2.3 Sign on farmland on a country road near Goldsboro, North Carolina

Figure 2.4 Urban graffiti in Atlanta, Georgia, 1990s

3

JEZEBEL REVAMPED[1]

Introduction

Southern women in the United States define Jezebel:[2] everything negative; wicked; scheming; whore; cheap harlot; either promiscuous or a complete whore; female form of gigolo; the name has seductive connotations; biblical queen; wife of Ahab; gave her husband bad advice; evil and treacherous; two-faced; one who seduces men and leads them to destruction; a woman who gets around; not ashamed; bimbo; I didn't know what it meant until my roommate called me this; someone who is wild, free, and comfortable with her sexuality; uninhibited, some might say slutty; a beautiful name; a southern belle with a mind and will and sex drive who is damned for not fitting the stereotype of a helpless, frigid woman; Scarlett O'Hara; Bette Davis in the red hoop dress in the 1938 film; condescending term used for African American women in the time of slavery; Gene loves Jezebel; you're a jezebel = flirty girl, light, flighty, aloof or dirty slut; free spirit, happy, cute, very feminine; always a lady (but not always nice); slinky; powerful; ambitious; calculating; ruthless; eaten by dogs; taking pleasure from material things; self-centered; decorated woman; painted face; *Cosmo* clothes; sensual; she has been given a "bad rep" by many scholars and people; she is famous for her badness; vamp, vampire, temptress, femme fatale, siren, witch – a woman who takes or ruins the life of another.

The body of the dead and defeated Jezebel in 2 Kings 9 and Apocalypse of John 2 returns in multiple texts as the classic femme fatale. Jezebel is the vamp/ire who roams the texts of culture and gender relations. The point in this chapter is not to reconstruct or re-form the biblical image of Jezebel, but to trace the trace of "jezebel" through various texts from the biblical period to the present using theories of intertextuality and the social construction of the body of the dead woman.

The complex and ambiguous character of Jezebel in the Bible serves as the archetypal bitch-witch-queen in misogynist representations of women. Beginning in 1 Kings 16 through 2 Kings 9 and reappearing again in Apocalypse 2: 20, Jezebel is the contradictory, controlling, carnal foreign woman. The common pronouncement (still widely used in the contemporary southern United States), "She is a regular Jezebel," underlies the imagining of Jezebel beginning with the Apocalypse 2: 20 passage and has referred to countless women from political queens including Mary Tudor, Mary Stuart, and Isabella I to movie queens such as Bette Davis, Vivian Leigh, and Elizabeth Taylor.

A sampling from different older and more recent biblical commentaries confirms this view of Jezebel as sexually evil and a demon woman: Ahab's "evils... are laid at her door... she came near to bringing the house of David to extinction" (Culver 1975: 589–90). She totally disregarded Israelite law and custom. To these more common reactions add: "She was a *woman of masculine temperament* and swayed her husband at will" (Gehman 1970: 492).[3] Jezebel is the foreign influence that is dangerous and brings destruction. In considering Jezebel, her reputation precedes her, regardless of how narrow or misogynist its presentation.

The Woman's Bible of 1895 turns to another dimension of Jezebel:

> Jezebel was a brave, fearless, generous woman, so wholly devoted to her own husband that even wrong seemed justifiable to her, if she could thereby make him happy. (In that respect she seems to have entirely fulfilled the Southern Methodist's ideal of the pattern wife entirely fulfilled in her husband.)
>
> (Stanton 1974: 75)

Jezebel is the equal rival of Elijah; both their deeds of genocide are seen as "savage" (Stanton 1974: 75).[4] The newer women's bible states that Jezebel "met her death with characteristic audacity: she painted her eyes, adorned her head, and greeted Jehu from her window with a caustic insult" (Exum 1985: 489).

I am "re-vamping" the generally accepted view of Jezebel as an evil woman from the biblical to the modern representations of her. Using theories on intertextuality from Bakhtin to Thibault and contemporary film theory, I trace the relations between the biblical text and other texts (drama, poetry, film, and art). The codes and "signifying practices" of the presence of Jezebel in a variety of texts have implications for the hermeneutics of gender and sexuality. In other words, the "trace" of Jezebel is in her adorned face peering through the lattice (representing the face of the goddess Asherah), with the image of her corpse as a vivid reminder of the defeat of the goddess-centered cultures – "they found no more of her than the skull and the feet and the palms of her hands" (2 Kgs. 9: 35). The text of the goddess is distorted and placed in only negative terms. I do not intend to un/recover a heroic woman figure from the biblical narrative or to redeem a "bad" woman of the Bible. I want to deal with the cultural representations and the interactions of readers with the image of Jezebel. A re-reading of different texts of Jezebel reveals the complexities of "that cursed woman" who fought to retain her indigenous culture and the continuation of the "curse" for all women who claim autonomy – sexual, religious, or political.

Jezebel

"Jezebel" has ambiguous definitions: from "unexalted, unhusbanded; or the brother is prince" (Gehman 1970: 492) or "where is the prince?" (Exum 1985: 489)[5] to meaning "*chaste* as does the common European name Agnes – quite inappropriate" (Culver 1975: 589). "Jezebel" means the monstrous female – loose and let loose, loose woman.[6] Why is the monster, here the jezebel, so fascinating? What is the "seduction," the draw into the dangerous darkness where the "monster" lurks?

Like the use of the "curse on Ham" as a justification for slavery of Africans, "jezebel" was the designation of the sexually dangerous African American slave woman. The juxtaposition of the images of the mammy and the jezebel served as an apologetic for the exploitation of the female slave. Deborah White (1985)[7] describes these divisions in terms of the madonna–whore dichotomy: the mammy is asexual; loving; warm; maternal; dark-skinned; big; older; wears formless clothes; covers her hair with a kerchief; is loyal, religious, and pious. The jezebel is sexual; provocative; young; with changing skin color; comely; promiscuous; provocatively dressed; a breeder; rebellious; a whore.

The white masters created these images to control and dominate the female slave. The mammy represents the desire for a positive image for African Americans. The jezebel was an excuse – of masters to justify their own adolescent and later adulterous behavior. White women blamed the jezebels in order to deny the rape and oppression of slave women. The jezebel acted out of the constraints of race and gender. The cultural "Africanisms" – of women having children before marriage and of exposing more of their bodies in the field as they worked – were misunderstood by whites. The whole system was based on the white male, which left white women finding ways to discredit the slave women.

So jezebel is not an abstract sign but a real physical presence – for antebellum culture and also in popular culture in the United States. Can one get outside the popular culture meaning of Jezebel?

Re-vamped

Recent biblical scholarship reveals the ambiguity of the character Jezebel and the religious/political rather than sexual intention of her painted face in the murder scene. But the term "jezebel" has distinct social meaning that is biblical (in Hosea; Ezekiel 16; the "strange woman" of Proverbs; the false prophetess of Apocalypse 2). Whoring and fornication are associated with strange religion and strange culture. Claudia Camp remarks that in the story of Naboth's vineyard, the Deuteronomic historian may have blamed Jezebel for Ahab's deed: "shifting of the blame to the foreign woman forms part of that era's polemic on the dangers of intermarriage" (1992: 104).[8] The jezebel schemes with both her mind and body. She has "been around" – in/from foreign territory (Tyre; Africa), and she brings danger with her. Therefore, her body must be destroyed. Look closely at the remains: skull; feet; palms of her hands (2 Kgs. 9: 35).

Viewing the dead body

The image of Jezebel is difficult to identify iconographically; her portrait and scenes of her life are rare.[9] Still, she is imaged as the temptress. Both men and women are drawn to her. Even though 2 Kgs. 9: 37 pronounces that "no one can say, This is Jezebel," the irony is that "This is Jezebel" is exactly what people said ever since this Deuteronomic proverb. The best view of the death scene is in Gustave Doré's *La Sancta Bible* in the print, *Les Compagnons de Jéhu Retrouvent la Tête et les Extremités de Jézabel*. The eye of the viewer is drawn to the central image of Jezebel's severed head, peacefully beautiful in its silence and separation from her body. The severed head is veiled here; in the picture of the previous scene of Jezebel

Figure 3.1 Detail from *The Death of Jezebel* (1865) by Gustave Doré

Figure 3.2 Detail from *Jehu's Companions Finding the Remains of Jezebel* (1865) by Gustave Doré: "But when they went to bury her, they found no more of her than the skull and the feet and the palms of her hands" (2 Kgs. 9: 35)

Figure 3.3 Detail from the Flemish Apocalypse (*c.* 1400 CE): Jezebel and her followers in bed together (Apoc. 2: 22)

Source: Bibliothèque Nationale, Paris.

being thrown out of the window by the eunuchs, *Jéhu Fait Précipiter Jézabel*, her hair is loose. The viewer is face-to-face with Jezebel. Does death bring her back to a virginal state? Is this face the death mask of the ideal woman? Is the ideal woman a dead woman – silent, fragmented, and powerless? Is the viewer responsible for her death? Is this the severed head of Medusa, a warning, a marker to other women who seek power?

In Doré's vision Jezebel's two hands and one foot remain. Whereas her head is covered, the hands and feet are exposed and thereby eroticized.[10] There is no blood and no corpus; only the extremities remain. The hands and foot seem to gesture. In her reading of "Rembrandt's" drawing of the Levite's wife on the threshold in Judges 19, Mieke Bal states, "The hand of this woman is crucial: it tells about death and about representation. It does not 'see,' but it speaks about mis-seeing.... It demonstrates that her gesture is phatic, enforcing semiosis" (1991: 370–1). So Jezebel's hands in the Doré drawing are poised and regal, even inviting. This Jezebel has been dis-abled, immobilized; her life (and evil doings) interrupted. In the sexual politics of the death scene by Doré the soldiers dominate; they stand over her transfixed, while one of them lifts her severed head for viewing. All that is left are the outermost parts. Why these body parts? These remains seem excessive, some textual excess – the excess of horror? – the excess of desire?

Jezebel's dead body parts are the signs of the liminal body, made even more liminal by their being dung on the fields. No one owns this body; as a king's daughter she is denied the appropriate burial by the dogs who eat her. Jezebel the Queen is now Jezebel the dog food. Her flesh is devoured. Jeze-baal/Asherah is eaten. "The corpse of Jezebel shall be like dung" (2 Kgs. 9: 37) shows the shaming and utter destruction of the Canaanite/Phoenician religion. The focus on scatology appears again in Jehu's destruction of a temple of Baal in 2 Kgs. 10: 27: "Then they demolished the pillar of Baal, and destroyed the temple of Baal, and made it a latrine to this day." A similar scatological joke is made at the Mount Carmel contest (1 Kgs. 18: 17). The reference to dung, outhouses, and a Canaanite god's deposal point to a way to dismiss and shame the enemy by referring to them by particular body parts (the Philistines as the uncircumcised ones) or by/as their body functions. Jezebel as dung represents the ultimate impurity. Thus, Jezebel and her religion are excrement to be excreted.

What is left of Jezebel is more than the sum of the dead body parts. In the horror of the death scene and the gaze of the viewer on the public execution – the fall, splattering blood, trampling horses, eating dogs, leftover flesh – the death of the female is forcefully presented. According to Virginia Allen in her study of the femme fatale, "Dead women, exotic women, embody a fierce and total rejection of living women" (1983: 186). Of course, Ahab also died a miserable, public death with the dogs drinking his blood. Ahab followed the evil ways of many kings before and after him, but he was "urged on by his wife Jezebel" (1 Kgs. 22: 25). The representation of Jezebel's death is different. She represents the power behind the throne, both political and spiritual. Her scattered body parts are a gendered focal point for the viewer, and their seductive power in Doré is intact. The power and seduction of Jezebel linger. Even after the destruction of the house of Ahab (especially Jezebel's daughter Athaliah, 2 Kgs. 11), Asherah returns, and Jezebel returns. So again, are the body parts markers, signs of warning: beware of foreign women and queen mothers; beware of all living women?

Despite warning, Jezebel returns eternally as vamp/ire, the phantom-ghost who roams time haunting both men and women. Jezebel is the vamp/ire that cannot be killed, who roams through other texts and times and women. She has a future in a different form; she is constantly re-formed in the image of male desire and fear. The "original" Jezebel is tangled up in its cultural texts, including the biblical story, that is its own invention of Jezebel. All texts of Jezebel are copies (Baudrillard's *simulacra*). Who's telling the truth? Everyone is. And no one is. Even the severed head speaks in tongues: tongues that are political, queenly, indigenous, elite, evil, religious, female, sexualized, monogamous, mothering, and murdered. The head speaks in the tongues of all the "texts" of Jezebel. The biblical text presents both the limits of Jezebel and her limitlessness. From the confines of her house she is the anti-prophet to Elijah the prophet (cf. Apoc. 2: 20). Jezebel talks to Jehu from her high window within female space. When she enters the male world, she is thrown to her death. Crossing that boundary is her last act – in the Deuteronomic text.

The intertext of desire

Jezebel is a fantasy space. She is an effect, a personality, a lifestyle, an ethical way of being female in the world, and an intertextual turn for the worst. Her multiple stories are parodies, including the biblical story. As parody, the Jezebel "texts" are ironic, contradictory, ambiguous, and paradoxical. Postmodern theorist Linda

Hutcheon equates parody with intertextuality. Hutcheon relates: "It [parody] is also not ahistorical or de-historicizing.... Instead, through a double process of installing and ironizing, parody signals how present representations come from past ones and what ideological consequences derive from both continuity and difference" (1988: 93). The biblical Queen Jezebel is reconsidered with each subsequent "text." There is no closure to the story of Jezebel's death in 2 Kings; as parody, Jezebel engages the reader in a montage of images.

Tom Robbins re-creates a parody of a modern Jezebel/Salome in his book, *Skinny Legs and All*, by questioning the tradition handed down in Western culture. The main character, Ellen Cherry, thinks to herself:

> What had Queen Jezebel done to earn the distinction as our all-time treacherous slut: In the Bitch Hall of Fame, Jezebel had a room of her own; nay, an entire wing. For fixing her hair and applying makeup? Was it implied that she went to the window to *flirt* with the rebel warrior? And if so, was that so wicked that it should wreck her reputation for three thousand years? The trimillennial lash bat?
>
> As Ellen Cherry walked the rain-rippled pavement of Seattle, bumpershooting from restaurant to restaurant in search of a job, she bore upon her back the weight of a skull, a pair of feet, and the palms of two hands. The nails of the feet were lacquered vermilion, a pretty ribbon fluttered from a lacuna in the skull. And she would wonder as she walked, "What is the Bible trying to tell us?"
>
> That Satan is a hairdresser?
>
> That Elizabeth Arden ought to be fed to the poodles?
>
> (Tom Robbins 1990: 33)[11]

Robbins is a lover of Jezebel, and his book is about his experience of *jouissance*. He plugs into the tradition of Jezebel as the ultimate femme fatale and creates a parody out of this web of desire. Jezebel's grave is empty; she stalks new victims in creative ways, forever crossing boundaries and challenging convention.

Mieke Bal points to the Jezebel narrative as an "ideo-story"; that is, a story taken out of context. Bal gives the example of a tabloid story, "Devilish Ladies Who Everybody Loves to Hate," which includes "Lilith, Jezebel, Delilah, and... Sappho.... The combination of the four figures is a function of the principle of coherent reading…. Both within and between the four stories, contradictions and problems are repressed" (1988: 11). That Delilah is not a liar or that Jezebel is not an adulteress get lost in the ideo-story. The reproduction of popular mythology is a priority in the reading process.

This reading of Jezebel in predominantly sexual terms is socially grounded. A social semiotics which draws from Bakhtin's heteroglossia is useful reading for Jezebel. The textual voices on Jezebel are many; they overlap, origins unknown (except the general patriarchal culture which is women's context). Paul Thibault promotes a "neomaterialist social semiotic," uniting theory and practice into the study of semiotics.[12] Thibault is involved in asking ethical questions of theory – that intertextual theorizing challenges existing hegemonic relations. In other words, intertextuality is grounded in a social context/community with certain dominant assumptions about how the world operates. The sign "jezebel" is embedded in social relationships and in a range of "texts." As John Frow states, "Texts are therefore not structures of presence by traces and tracings of otherness. They are shaped by the repetition and the transformation of other textual structures" (1990: 45). Jezebel is not an image but *images*, a plural form.

The whoring Jezebel is of course the most seductive image. In discussing seduction and prostitution in Flaubert, Ross Chambers writes: "In the homosocial world, literature must pose, in order to gain acceptance, as a figure of powerlessness, helpless or charming: a child or a woman…. Literature, in short, must camp it up" (1990: 155). Thus, the passage in Apocalypse 2 stands out: Jezebel refuses to repent and continues to beguile and fornicate. "Beware, I am throwing her on a bed, and those who commit adultery with her I am throwing into great distress, unless they repent of her doings; and I will strike her children dead" (Apoc. 2: 22–3). And the Jezebel in 2 Kings 9 paints her face and fixes her hair boldly to face death and the fulfillment of the prophecy of the enemy. What would the apocalyptic Jezebel say to the narrator John in reply? What would Queen Jezebel say to the narrator of her life story? Are their only traces skull and feet and palms of the hands and dead children?

An outside Jezebel has invaded the text, a Jezebel who would proclaim (as did Ellen Cherry's cynical mother Patsy in *Skinny Legs and All*), "Of the Seven Deadly Sins, lust is definitely the pick of the litter" (1990: 106). But the biblical Jezebel does not seek or find sexual pleasure. Looking out the lattice, Jezebel is framed. She is also imprisoned. In the biblical text, as well as in early twentieth-century "devotional fiction," Jezebel is a prisoner in her own palace; she never leaves or confronts men (like Elijah) on the outside. Jezebel remains inside; acting behind the lattice. All attempts to colonize her fail.

The colonial nature of the jezebel text and the oppression of the jezebel voice are apparent in the sadistic retelling of her death. In her book on the effects of imperialism on the reading process, Laura Donaldson calls for a "materialist-feminist semiotics" that "requires that we not only recognize how micrologies of power keep certain information systems in place while simultaneously suppressing others but also resist the temptation of an unmediated politics of meaning" (1992: 120–1). The discourse on Jezebel is guided through the colonial mind. The image of the Other, the foreign, the dangerous, and thereby seductive woman is used against medieval women and slave women and southern women who break with tradition. Tom Robbins attempts to decolonize Jezebel:

> Jezebel. Jezebel. Painted Queen of Israel. I am praising thee, O Queen of Israel. Whore of the Golden Calf. Strumpet of Baal. Jezebel. Slut of Samaria. Our queen whom the dogs are eating. The watercourse of the Jews is flowing through thee. Jezebel. My Queen. Whose daughter is ruling in Jerusalem. From whose womb is pouring the House of David. Mmm. Jezebel. Priestess of Fornication. Mmm. Queen of Spades. Queen of Tarts. O Jezebel, you are my queen, I exalt thee and praise thy sandals.
>
> (Robbins 1990: 348)

Even though in popular Western culture to be called a jezebel is not a compliment, there is a strange connection/disconnection to Jezebel. Women read themselves as Jezebel, as having the "jezebel spirit."[13] Are we happy/satisfied when Jezebel is splattered and trampled by horses and eaten by dogs? What have we done with the story of Jezebel? Is her story continually recolonized, re-opened, the brief scenes of her life re-enacted and reinscribed?

4

THE POWER OF BABEL: SPIRALING OUT OF CONTROL

I live in Atlanta, Georgia, home of Coca-Cola. The Coke building downtown is a Tower of Babel for me, once towering over the oldest public housing project in the United States, until the Olympic Village displaced the poor who lived in the shadows of Coke. The classic drink bottle itself is a tower, as Andy Warhol noted in his pop artwork of the repetition of Coke, *Green Coca-Cola Bottles* (1962) now at the Whitney Museum. Coke also has a museum in Atlanta, "The World of Coca-Cola," a grand fetish to the sweet, sticky drink. This museum is about the ideology of Coke: one world, one ontology (Coke = "the real thing"), one drink, one language, one harmony ("I'd like to teach the world to sing, in perfect harmony"). At the Coke Museum at the end, you can drink any of about fifty or so different "Cokes" from different countries. Each "Coke" is made with slightly different recipes, yet they are all "Coke." Babel bursts into Pentecost, and the tourists are sent forth full of "Coke."

Cokes, like Babel, are produced by human laborers. Like Coke, Babel is a building and a body – a body of culture, a body of desire, a desired body. The boycotts of Coke that certain peace and justice groups have called for in recent years point to the oppression of workers by multinational corporations in Third World countries such as Guatemala. Bodies build the tower, the tower of bodies reaches for God, for the real thing. The cost of Babel is human bodies, piles of bodies. Underlying the desire to be equal to God and to create structures to reach God are structures of oppression.

In the Genesis 11 story God and humans meet, although this meeting is not a democratic dialogue. Edward Said says, "For the linguist, language cannot be pictured as the result of force emanating unilaterally from God" (1978: 136), and in this story the language of Eden is scattered into many. And God exerts force by scattering the (subversive?) talk. Perhaps the Babel workers decided to unionize or to plan a movement to storm heaven. The story spirals off as the tower does, into the heavens, and then, in most artist representations, into ruin. Humans are left to figure out how to build coalitions in these ruins.[1]

Babel falls in the center of the biblical trinity of creation-confusion-chaos. Is the shape of the tower itself a trinity, a triangle? The world is created out of the deep chaotic female space – "God saw that it was good." Then the drama and tension builds as human creatures strive/spiral to connect with or be the creator. The spiraling snake pronounces the path that leads to the divinity to the woman. The mother tongue is repressed, then scattered. Elaine Scarry relates, "Human acts of building, making, creating, working are throughout the Old Testament surrounded with layer upon layer of prohibition from above and inhibition from below" (1985: 221). The Babylonians are surrounded by God's power. Are we as readers supposed to take God's side in this story?

Babel is, in Scarry's words, "a scene of wounding" (1985: 200). She states:

> As God in the scene of hurt is a bodiless voice, so men and women are voiceless bodies. God is their voice; they have none separate from him. Repeatedly, any capacity for self-transformation into a separate verbal or material form is shattered, as God shatters the building of the Tower of Babel by shattering the language of the workers into multiple and mutually uncomprehending tongues.
>
> (1985: 200)

Scarry also notes that, "The vocabulary of punishment describes the event only from the divine perspective, obscures the use of the body to make experienceable the metaphysical abstraction whose remoteness has occasioned disbelief" (1985: 201). At the end of time tongues either sing for joy or fall silent. One of the things the damned do is gnaw their tongues (Apoc. 16: 10). There is no language for the damned but a gnawed agony. Babel is the story of one of the primeval punishments, another way God remains separate from humans. Babel is a story of prime-evil religion and culture and of wounding and pain.

When I first thought about possible feminist readings of the

Figure 4.1 The Confusion of Tongues (1865) by Gustave Doré: the people mourn as they are scattered from the spiraling tower – the possibility of divine desire

Tower of Babel narrative, I thought of the tower image as a male phallic symbol. Mary Daly sees the tower as "the erection of phallocracy" (1978: 4). Women have to "break through this multiple barrier composed of deceptions ejaculated by 'God'..." to reach "the Gates of the Goddess" (1978: 4). There is also a kind of castration in God's ending the building project by scattering the people. Slavoj Žižek says in his discussion of "the problem of 'real Genesis'" that difference as pain (Heidegger) "points towards the materialist problematic of the traumatic cut, 'castration,' which marks our entry into language" (1994a: 129). Further, Žižek uses Schelling to contrast the coming of the *logos* out of the abyss and how human ego is in conflict with God's outpouring love: "This unbearable antagonism is timelessly past, a past that was never 'present,' since the present already implies *logos*, the clearing of the spoken Word that transposes the antagonistic pulsation of the drives into the symbolic difference" (1994a: 129). Žižek reasons:

> God cannot be reduced to *logos*, there is something in Him which is not Reason, Word, namely the obscure foundation of His existence, what is in God "more than Himself," the Real in God; this is why the presentation of the content of the Absolute must assume the form of a narration, of a story about God's "ages" that goes beyond rendering the inner necessity of a network of pure logical determinations.
>
> (1994a: 211)

Babel's destruction creates monsters (especially Nimrod) that spring from the wounded space. Augustine envisioned "monstrous humanoids" at the Tower in *The City of God* 16.8 (see Jeffrey 1992: 66). According to this supreme patriarchal reading, Babel houses monsters. It is best to keep clear of its gates, its siren call, its seductive presence.

There are many stories similar to the Genesis Babel that raise these issues. Consider an Ashanti myth from Africa entitled, "The Tower to Heaven," that is similar to the Babel story:

> Long, long ago Onyankopon lived on earth, or at least was very near to us. Now there was a certain old woman who used to pound her mashed yams and the pestle kept knocking up against Onyankopon, who was not then high up in the sky. So Onyankopon said to the old woman, "Why do you keep doing this to me? Because of what you

are doing I am going to take myself away up in the sky."
And of a truth he did so.

Now the people could no longer approach Onyankopon.
But the old woman thought of a way to reach him and
bring him back. She instructed her children to go and
search for all the mortars they could find and bring them to
her. Then she told them to pile one mortar on top of
another till they reached to where Onyankopon was. And
her children did so, they piled up many mortars, one on top
of another, till they needed only one more mortar to reach
Onyankopon.

Now, since they could not find another mortar
anywhere, their grandmother the old woman said to them:
"Take one out from the bottom and put it on top to make
them reach." So her children removed a mortar from the
bottom and all the mortars rolled and fell to the ground,
causing the death of many people.

(Feldman 1963: 41–2)

In this African myth the desire for the connection with the god
causes death.

In a contemporary fantasy version of the Tower of Babel by James
Morrow, God decides that unifying all the languages will bring
more chaos. In a reverse Babel, God decides that clarity will cause
the world's people to resort back to a stone-age style of life, thus
ending the mad capitalism that will ultimately destroy the earth.
God sets up his plan by moving into a skyscraper in New York City
owned by the wealthiest man in the world, Daniel Nimrod (biblical
reference in the last name intended). God describes his actions: "As
divine retributions go, it was surely My most creative work since
the locusts, lice, flies, murrain, blood, boils, dead children, hail,
frogs, and darkness. And here's the kicker, people: I did it with
language alone" (1996: 62). When everyone can understand
everyone else, earth becomes a place where "Half the planet is now a
graduate seminar, the other half a battleground" (1996: 83). There
is no longer the striving for "arrogant space shuttles or presump-
tuous particle accelerators" (1996: 84). There is no nuance in
language and there are no untranslatable tongues. God speaks, and,
"To their utter bewilderment and total horror, they know that
nothing is being lost in translation" (1996: 83). Morrow turns the
Babel story inside out; what if the peoples on earth suddenly spoke
in the same language? The erasure of this difference leads to

disunity, not unity. The tower God opposes is one like the Trump Tower, where the excess of the real estate mogul imagining he is God is reconfigured. The tower is a giant phallus symbol of humanity's greed, and the city of New York represents Babylon's classist state.

I want to take off from these stories in a different direction. I want to propose that the Tower of Babel is a phallic symbol, but not a male one. Again I want to draw from African creation mythology and propose that the Tower of Babel is similar to the termite hill in the Dogon myth of creation. In other words, the tower is the erect female clitoris wounded by God. There is castration but it is female genital mutilation, as in the Dogon myth. This myth states: "Amma brought an earth woman to arise from a lump of clay. Her clitoris was made of a termite hill. When Amma tried to unite with her, the termite hill barred his way by asserting her masculinity. Amma defeated the rebellious termite hill; he cut off the obstacle and united himself with the excised earth." The philosophy behind this myth is as follows:

> If the child is a boy the female principle will dwell on the foreskin; in case of a girl, the male principle will reside in the clitoris.... The purpose of the rites of circumcision and excision is to force the individual to lean definitely toward the one of the two principles for which his body is the better suited.
>
> (Feldman 1963: 68)

In *Possessing the Secret of Joy* (and in the film, *Warrior Marks*) Alice Walker uses this myth to define religion as "an elaborate excuse for what man has done to women and the earth" (1993a: 99, 235). The erect clitoris is a threat to male power and domination. Eco relates that "In the opinion of various Arab authors... the confusion was due to the trauma induced by the sight, terrifying no doubt, of the collapse of the tower" (1995: 9). Perhaps the tower represents female desire for connection with the divine, like Eve's desire. Perhaps this desire is as in Greek mythology – women's search for full sexual fulfillment. The open top of the tower in Pieter Bruegel's images is clitoral-shaped. Is the top of the tower a mouth, with lips to speak in a unified language to the deity? (cf. Isa. 55: 12). The root of the English words "tongue," "language," and "lingo" have the same root, *dnghu*, "tongue" (*American Heritage Dictionary*: 1047). Mouth and mountain share the root "men" which means "to project"; other meanings from the root include: menace, projecting points, threats, threaten, jut (*American Heritage Dictionary*: 2114). Perhaps the top of the tower/mountain/mouth is menacing/threatening to the deity (cf. Ezek. 6: 3–4, 36). The tower jutting into the gate of God would be the ultimate violation of God's power. This space cannot be shared on equal terms. The division between humans and deity must be clearly, violently marked. The Babel text has echoes of violence, echoes of violation; in the Bible, God responds to the female desire to penetrate heaven by penetrating the female with part of heaven in Luke 1: 26–38 and Apocalypse 12.

The traditional idea of the reasoning behind the builders' actions is that they were acting out of pride, hubris. Derrida has a different take on the actions of the tower builders, mainly that "they want to impose their lip on the entire universe. Had their enterprise succeeded, the universal tongue would have been a particular language imposed by violence, by force, by violent hegemony over the rest of the world" (1985: 101). Babel becomes the proper name given by God the Father. The "confusion" at Babel is that God wants humans to translate his proper name into a "common noun" because his name is untranslateable (1985: 102). God wins the war of impositions by deconstructing the tower and imposing his name

Figure 4.2 Detail from *The Small Tower* (1563) by Pieter Bruegel the Elder

on humans.[2] The lips of the mouth of Babel kiss the sky and almost kiss the deity. Babel is a goddess, built to be the consort of the most high God. Babel is an idol, or in Michel Serres' words, a Leviathan:

> Here is that massive, colossal animal called Leviathan, or 666, a Babel in flesh and fleece. We are not really sure if this organism is viable, we only know that it is monstrous. God, evil, I do not know, misshapen in every instance.
>
> (1995: 124)

The tower as 666, the number of the triple goddess of North Africa, has become a monster in this reading of Babel. Augustine rants about "monstrous humanoids" in his discussion of the Tower of Babel (*The City of God* 16.8, in Jeffrey 1992: 66). Independent women (and goddesses) are called towers of Babel. Babel and Babylon represent "a concentrated embodiment of the forces of chaos" (Cohn 1993: 153, 217). Babel, chaos, abyss.

The scattering is not just about language but about desexing the female. And these myths are from very different cultures. But then Babel is the city Babylon which is eventually represented as a whore who is stripped, gang raped, killed, eaten and burned forever. The city as female – or the female as city – never fares well in the Bible. Her sexual power is always under control, made passive or destroyed. Herodotus reports that the god of the Babylonians would choose one woman to go into the shrine of one of the great towers and be shut in for the night. Herodotus states, "These same Chaldaeans say (but I do not believe them) that the god himself is wont to visit the shrine and rest upon the couch... and neither the Egyptian nor the Babylonian woman, it is said, has intercourse with men...." In this room with a couch and a golden table the god has intercourse with the woman (I: 181–2). A woman is placed at the top of the tower for the god to visit; is this a story of sacred prostitution or divine rape? Are supernatural children ever born from this relationship (as in Gen. 6: 1–4)? Is this Babel Tower the spiraling snake of wisdom and female power, once again the desires (of the ancient goddess traditions?) punished by God? The spiraling of the tower in the iconography is the spiraling image in goddess traditions and women's ritual power (the spiral dance). Why play with the tower image as female desire? Irigaray opens the possibilities further:

To play with mimesis is thus, for a woman, to try to recover the place of her exploitation by discourse, without allowing herself to be simply reduced to it. It means to resubmit herself – inasmuch as she is on the side of the "perceptible," of "matter" – to "ideas," in particular to ideas about herself, that are elaborated in/by a masculine logic, but so as to make "visible," by an effect of playful repetition, what was supposed to remain invisible: the cover up of a possible operation of the feminine in language.

(Irigaray 1985: 76, quoted/discussed in Butler 1993: 47)

The spiraling tower repeats itself; the site of the ruins (in the art of the tower) repeats the site of punishment.

Eco traces the history of art on Babel and notes that beginning in the eleventh century was created, "the story of how a real wound had been inflicted on humanity, a wound that might, in some way, be healed once more" (1995: 17). Pieter Bruegel the Elder's coliseum-like Babel Tower shows the open wound that gapes open toward the future. W.J.T. Mitchell takes a different position: "The point, then, is not to heal the split between words and images, but to see what interests and powers it serves" (1986: 44). The art of the tower incorporates the body. Human bodies are the tower's building material in a painting by Stanislao Lepri from 1965 and in Cobi Reiser's representation of 1967 (Minkowski 1991: 264–5). In Lepri's tower, nude human bodies construct and are the material for the tower. The people alternate in eight rows facing and turning their backs on the viewer. Each layer of people stands on a platform held up by the people below. The expressions on their faces are fuzzy but look pained. On the third row one person is slipping off the platform and is barely helped up by another. This structure defies the laws of physics and accentuates the theme of burden. There is human cost to building Babel, from the slave laborers of the ancient world to the artistic representations of bodies spiraling toward heaven, heavy under the burden of their own desire. Thus, the body is marginalized in the Bible and there are many "scenes of wounding," and I think Babel is one of those scenes. God is a transgressor, or as the *Book of J* translation has Yahweh saying, "They conceive this between them, and it leads up until no boundary exists to what they will touch.... From there Yahweh scattered them over the whole face of earth; the city there came unbound" (Bloom and Rosenberg 1990: 73). Gustave Doré's scene of the aftermath of the scattering features in the forefront an anguished man

Figure 4.3 Tower of Babel (1965) by Stanislao Lepri

Figure 4.4 Tower made of bodies (*c.* 1967) by Cobi Reiser

Figure 4.5 Lotte Medelsky as "Frau Welt" (summer 1931) in the Salzburg
Theatre

with arms raised toward heaven (see Minowski 1991: 247; cf. Hugo Lou Mohr, in Minowski 1991: 256). In a volcanic inverse of the abyss, human creation arises and partially falls; the people flee from their attempt at "paradise."

The response to the wounding is often a gendered response. In a whimsical turn, an actress dons a Babel Tower hat in her role as Mrs World in Salzburg in 1931 (Minowski 1991: 247). The hat is a sort of taunt to the deity; a mini-attempt to breach the heavens. Is the Tower of Babel female sexuality out of control? Is the tower the monstrous-feminine (Kristeva)? The body of the deep out of which the first discourse emerged that must be bound and destroyed by God, as Marduk destroyed Tiamat? For Mary Doane, "The positing of a body *is* a condition of discursive practices" (1988: 226). Is it also a place of cultural and divine politics? I think there is an "exegesis of erotics" or "erotic exegesis" that can be done with Genesis 11; in other words, there is an erotic component to the narrative.

Art for utopia's sake

Herodotus describes that the way up to the tower is spiral, with benches for resting along the way (I: 181–2). Some (especially earlier) art has the workers building the tower undisturbed. But in much art on the Tower of Babel the top of the tower is either unfinished or destroyed and crumbling. Sometimes God (and often also angels) hang down from heaven and intervene in the building process. One example is the *c.* 1340 print in the Welislaw Bible, which shows God with a long-handled instrument picking up a top brick; two angel arms use the same tool to pull workers off the building (Minowski 1991: 26–7). In fifteenth-century art from the Netherlands sometimes the angels descend and people scatter (e.g. Cornelis Anthonisz, 1547), and sometimes the tower stands in a central position, with people worshipping a king off to one side (Pieter Bruegel the Elder, 1563) (see Minkowski 1991: 37, 39, 70, 71). In one modern painting by Cuno Fischer (1960) a pale hand comes down from heaven, almost touching the tower, while two shadowy human figures watch from below (Minkowski 1991: 102; cf. Franz Masereel's tower of 1964, Minkowski 1991: 258).

The tower has multiple forms and historical connections. Oftentimes the tower looks like the Coliseum in Rome (to represent political power), as in Pieter Bruegel the Elder's paintings (Weiner 1985: 210). Sarah Weiner notes that the multitude of fifteenth-century Babel paintings in the Netherlands is because of "their rele-vance to the major issues of the Dutch Revolt: the hegemony of the Roman Church and the tyranny of the Spanish monarchy" (1985: 6). The paintings of the tower are about punishment for human pride (Weiner 1985: 153). The Dutch emphasis was on the power of Rome (political and religious) and the fantastic story and architec-ture of Babylon/Rome. For Martin Luther, Rome is the Tower of Babel, and Latin was the unifying language until it was destroyed by Luther's movement.

In many paintings there is a Crucifixion scene in the back-ground; one prominent scene is in a miniature in a volume of Augustine's *The City of God* painted by Raoul de Praelles (1473–80) (Minkowski 1991: 146). Markus Lüpertz's *Babylon Diorama II* in 1941 shows the top of a tower as a cross (Minkowski 1991: 117). The medieval representations of the tower are a main source of information about medieval building practices (showing lots of pulleys and other building devices). In most representations the tower is the central, triangular piece in a lost utopian city. The violence of angels throwing workers off the tower and the scattered people are secondary components in the art. Most often, any people at the base of the tower are hanging around; in Gaspar Poyo de Torre's drawing of 1712–13 some people lie in poses of the leisure class, while others depart (Minkowski 1991: 225).

What I find in the paintings of the tower is desire – the desire for utopia, the desire to rebuild the tower. Literary utopias are places where racism and classism reign (e.g. Thomas More's *Utopia*; Charlotte Perkins Gilman's *Herland*; the 1939 Frank Capra film, *Lost Horizon*). The imaginary narratives behind the paintings bring these negative aspects of utopia to mind. Twentieth-century artist Robert Smithson emphasizes the spiraling utopic vision of the tower in his *Spiral Jetty* site piece on Great Salt Lake, Utah – a labyrinth like the Bruegel and Escher respresentation of Babel, only Smithson's site piece is flat. The Tower of Babel is the main form behind much of Smithson's art. Gary Shapiro speculates that Smithson may have found the "lost prime" or prototype of the tower in the mythic city of Atlantis (1995: 259, n. 27). Smithson sometimes displaces Babel by building an "antimonument," such as the jetty, which is a ruin of Babel (Shapiro 1995: 101, 223). The *Spiral Jetty* represents the suburbs for Smithson; it is "some-thing like a deconstructed Tower of Babel that both exhibits and erases the signature of its maker" (Shapiro 1995: 226). *A Heap of Language* (1986) is a pencil drawing of a pyramid heap of words, beginning with "language." Shapiro notes "the artist's idea of the universe as a Babel of printed matter" (1995: 186), and that "in Babel there is nothing to do but shore up fragments, as Smithson learned from Eliot and Pound" (Shapiro 1995: 180). Since the artists of the Tower of Babel did not sign their work, Babel was doomed to ruin from the beginning: "When God destroyed the tower, he prevented them from signing their work and became the first deconstructive, entropic artist" (Shapiro 1995: 221). The square, spiral, flat and earth-bound fragments of Babel in Smithson's art ground the viewer in the garden (of Eden) but also show the tension in the language of the void (in the ruins) and of utopia (in the escape from the ruins).

Babel 2: beyond Babel (with a vengeance)

Imagining Babel as an archeological site

In other cultural representations of Babel/Babylon, it is reproduced as a spectacle of a transgressive place of perversion. The city is complete with a dominant whore (the Whore of Babylon), but the assumption (in art and film) is that everybody Babylonian is evil and perverse. The whore symbol combines capital economy and the female in "a bacchanalia of fetishism" residing in "the deviant sexual topology of Babylon" (Hansen 1991: 233). The city is the opposite of the ideal city of God, the New Jerusalem. Human pride and perversion cause God to act and destroy the tower and city, and all the inhabitants deserve what happens to them. Cultural representations of Babel/Babylon are rather anachronistic; in Genesis 11 there is no mention of perversion (or a gendered economy), and the city is not even completely built, for when God scatters them, "they left off building the city" (11: 9). But the art of Babel is certainly not literal; what is important is to tell a good story, one with which spectators will connect.

In D.W. Griffith's silent film *Intolerance* (1916) Babel/Babylon represents a universal language, as he considers the medium of film does. In particular, silent film allows the spectator to participate silently in the universal language. The actress Lillian Gish recalls:

> To me, *Intolerance* recalls Mr. Griffith's words: "We have gone beyond Babel, beyond words. We have found a new universal language, a power that can make men brothers

and end war forever. Remember that! Remember that when
you stand in front of a camera!"

(quoted in Hansen 1991: 173)

Griffith obviously had a utopian view of film. The fall of Babylon is
one of four separate stories in *Intolerance*, in which cities are places of
decadence and exploitation. All nations are at the feet of the city-
state Babylon, and Griffith is commenting on the Hollywood
Babylon in which he works, the perverse power base of the movie
industry.

In the film's Babylon the Tower of Babel is an archaeological
ruin. Griffith has a scene in which the Babylonian Nabonidus holds
up a brick he excavated from the Babel ruins of the Naram-Sin
temple of 3,200 years earlier. In this way "the Babylonian space is
already figured as an archaeological site, as a space of reconstruction" (Hansen 1991: 181). Griffith has rebuilt Babel in the form of
the universal language of (silent) film. The fall of Babel is a sign of a
new language (1991: 194). Hansen relates: "As an allegory of an
impossible unity and transparency, the Babylonian narrative also
dramatizes the impossibility of historical continuity. Repairing the
ruins of Babel requires an apocalyptic break…" (1991: 195). Several
films play on this theme of rebuilding the tower; *Metropolis* (Fritz
Lang 1926) and the cyberpunkish *Blade Runner* (Ridley Scott 1982,
which shares with Griffith an orientalist view). In all these films a
capitalist economy has gone wild; workers are exploited and the gap
between rich and poor is enormous. The commentary is that if left
unchecked, capitalism will bring dystopia, not utopia, and lead the
ideal vision of "America" to ruins.

In reading the film *Intolerance* Hansen notes that God caused the
destruction and dispersion out of jealousy and "intolerance." But
the idea/l of a universal language is a popular one: "If God's punishment has stamped this quest [for a universal language] as a
forbidden repetition, as mimicry and idolatry, it has likewise
perpetuated its utopian appeal" (Hansen 1991: 185). Hansen points
out the connection for Griffith with Babel and the World
Expositions of the turn of the century; the San Francisco Exposition
of 1915 had as its main feature the "Tower of Jewels" (1991: 237).
Griffith's film is a critique of the decadence and desire of American
culture in the early twentieth century and of "any society that uses
the threat of castration to perpetuate a system of economic, social,
and cultural deprivation" (1991: 239). The retelling of the story of
the ruins of Babel repeats the threat of castration: "Excising, cutting

out. What is your fear? That you might lose your property. What remains is an empty frame. You cling to it, dead" (Irigaray 1992: 24–5, quoted in Grosz 1995: 111).

The "Tower of Jewels" may immediately bring to mind the phallic reference to "the family jewels" of male genitalia. An interesting connection here is that, as Sue Best points out, *kletoris* (Gk) can also mean "jewel" or "gem" (1995: 39, n. 7). This reference might be interesting to pursue further in terms of materialist readings of the body and language.

The imaginary ruins of Babel – and Eden – fill the Western cultural canvases. Babel and bodies are both part of the scene in art; the bodies are building, fleeing, or being plucked off the tower by God. Dianne Chisholm offers an interesting way to read texts with the female body in mind in erotic literature. Lesbian erotic literature has reclaimed the female body. Chisholm suggests that litcrit reads for the phallus, while "litclit" reads for women's desire (1995: 34). She uses the term "cunning lingua" for the language system that stands "for the erogenous zone of partial body whose excitability/erectability is supposed to be the unmediated expression of desire." This linguistics is not a real organ "but a word-thing-act, a prosthesis composed of verbal matter, capable of forming, touching and arousing..." (1995: 24).[3] Is the building of Babel a symbol of erotic desire, the sexualizing of the sacred, the desire to rebuild/rebirth Eden and claim that space against a jealous God?

The Babel Tower is a container of language. Is it chora, that Platonic space between mind and body? The traditional dialectic goes: man is time and woman is space. Chora is female: "Woman is/provides space for man, but occupies none herself" (Grosz 1995: 99), and is how women are to relate in the social world.[4] So what did the Tower of Babel contain? The simple answer is "language," as in Robert Smithson's narrative drawing, *A Heap of Language* (1966) (see Shapiro 1995: 161). Deleuze would say the tower contained (and produced) the language of desire. In Marxist terms perhaps this language in Babel is the language of the superstructure of the economy; Genesis 11 raises the issue of slave labor and trade in the ancient economy. Is Babel (as chora) the mother of all towers? Best notes that feminizing of space "underscores an anxiety about this 'entity' and the precariousness of its boundedness" (1995: 183). This "heap of language" contained in female space is not safe space.

The return to the site of Babel is also evident in rock and roll music. Musician Patti Smith makes the connection between the babbling of ancient Egyptian priestesses and Christian glossolalia.

She describes that the merging of these two languages produces "a new rock language – BABYLOGUE – neither male nor female" (Graham 1993: 82). Smith sees rock and roll as the language of Babel and of women again babelling in religious ecstasy. Artist Dan Graham says about Smith as she portrayed a whirling dervish on stage: "She speculated on herself as a female GOD" (1993: 95). The repetition of the music, of the images of the pop artists provided a mesmerizing return to the ruins of Babel. These art forms of the avant-garde that reproduce Babel as the gate of God push toward the gate, repeating the act of desire in Genesis 11.

Rebuilding Babel

The tower is immense. According to the "poetics of space" of Bachelard, immensity or vastness is imagination or daydream of a space that is "elsewhere" (1969: 184). He finds the word "vast" in Baudelaire's poetry "...a word that brings calm and unity; it opens up unlimited space" (1969: 197). Bachelard quotes him on the power of immensity: "I felt freed from *the powers of gravity*, and, through memory, succeeded in recapturing the extraordinary *voluptuousness* that pervades *high places*... in other words, immensity with no other setting than itself" (1969: 195). Does the immense "tower with its top in the heavens" (Gen. 11: 4) represent a "voluptousness that pervades high places?" Do mountains and towers share in the symbolism of the spiritual search for the dwelling of the divine? The tower minimizes the immense *space* between humans and God for a brief moment in Genesis 11. The top of the tower is the frontier, the unexplored space, the outermost reaches, the limits, the margins of existence. When God scatters all the people the space regains its immensity.

Does the tower represent the excess of human desire and sensual pleasure, breaking through to heaven? Is there dual excess here: the human choice to build an immense tower and God's choice to disperse the people over all the earth? Where are the limits of human desire, and what if one imagines limitless desire? I am drawn by the statement God makes in Gen. 11: 6: "Look, they are one people, and they have all one language; and this is only the beginning of what they will do; nothing that they propose to do will now be impossible for them." God has already made the tree of immortality off limits. If the tower reaches heaven, then humans will be able to do anything – does this mean humans will share the power of God? If humans storm heaven, does this mean all humans,

slave laborers and rulers? I am curious about the "they" of Gen. 11:
3 – could "they" be the slave laborers who decide to storm heaven as
the last brick is laid? In the opera, *The Tower*, there is the conversation between the doctors and their patient, a woman named Ruth
who is undergoing an operation and dreaming of rebuilding the
Tower of Babel, and her husband, Jacob:

RUTH: My mouth is a kiln.
RAFEL, ZABI: I hear the bricks sing as they rise up.
AMEK, JACOB: And the right of revolt –
RUTH: Is embedded in the tower of my mouth.

(Maguire 1993: 37)

In this opera, Ruth's desire to rebuild the tower is linked with the
desire for the end of earthly violence. In the Babel story is the
spiraling tower a way to get back at God for the violence of the
flood and a way to avoid the prophecy that God will scatter them
(Gen. 11: 4) – a way of both making a name for themselves and a
way of storming heaven? Does the tower represent a utopian,
unified, and unconfused human hope for peace?

The class boundaries are confusing in the Babel story; is the
narrator sympathetic to the plight of the builders, linking the
desires of the reader with the desires in the text? Usually, Babylon is
clearly the "enemy Other" whose destruction or failure is to be
cheered (see Cohn 1993: 153). But in Genesis 11 the class of the
builders is not clear, and they seem to be part of a unified movement and language. Then they all get scattered, which means "my
people and tongue" are in there somewhere. So identification of the
enemy Babylon is not clear; in fact I find myself cheering for their
plight like it is some olympics of architecture, the ultimate prize of
which is heaven.

As a reader I am intrigued by the notion of "nothing they
propose to do will now be impossible for them" in a similar way as I
am curious about "he might reach out his hand and take also from
the tree of life, and eat, and live forever" (Gen. 3: 22) – it is like the
explorer de Soto searching for the fountain of youth daydream. God
thwarts human excess. God redefines this excess of human desire
and ability in the act of scattering the languages and peoples. There
is a limit to the excesses God will allow. In *The Tower* Jacob worries:
"Can you imagine a conspiracy to take over heaven? You'd have to
have meetings, and codes, and secret handshakes..." (Maguire 1993:
39). This contemporary Jacob also dreams of a ladder to heaven,

reminiscent of God and angels descending in Genesis 28, where the biblical Jacob proclaims, "This is none other than the house of God and this is the gate of heaven" (Gen. 28: 17). The ladder is another Babel/gate of God. In the opera, Jacob desires to climb the ladder to be with God, but God has confiscated all the ladders: "Piles of them in heaven's pound" (Maguire 1993: 54). He sees his wife Ruth's desire to rebuild Babel as the only alternative, for:

> then the Lord, the goddamn landlord of the envelope, will be forced to come to the table. Forced to negotiate. We want to be in Paradise. We want it. We deserve it. You bet your ass, it's Hubris. And about time. How many millennium we gonna scrape around the humble pen?
>
> (Maguire 1993: 55)

This Jacob deconstructs traditional notions of sin and hubris. In biblical and contemporary narratives, storming heaven is left to the world of fantasy. The human "quest of intimacy" that is part of immensity (Bachelard 1969: 195) that began with Eve cannot continue in this form of immense desire for connection with the divine.

The lead character Ruth in the opera, *The Tower*, pronounces her overwhelming desire to build the tower from its ruins: "The Babel of my body, / ... You won't catch me thinking twice, I'm climbing to paradise" (Maguire 1993: 45). Ruth calls this desire "her condition" to which her husband replies, "That's an understatement. You're a goddamn walking Tower of Babel" (Maguire 1993: 50). When Ruth dreams she breaks through to heaven she meets a white, bearded God with sharp teeth. They wrestle. God ("the Angry Avenging God") tries to rape her with his "prime patriarchal part, a real biblical number," but Ruth successfully fights him (Maguire 1993: 74). The opera ends with the desire in ruins – the ruins of the tower. Anyone who looks upon the ruins develops amnesia. Ruth describes the end of her desire: "I contained the memory, / wrapping the pain in layers, over and over, / so that it became / like a pearl" (Maguire 1993: 85). She can no longer speak the dream of the tower but finds strength in crossing the boundaries of waking and dreaming to remember the violence and the ruins.

This is clearly a stretch – but I like what Bachelard says about the vowel "a" in the word vast: "I begin to think that the vowel *a* is the vowel of immensity" (1969: 197). Some ancient philosophers claimed the original language was Hebrew, an ancient language of consonants. In *The Tower* Ruth proclaims: "in the beginning there were only consonants – and God's gift to Man in the garden was vowels – The Lord giveth and the Lord laugheth all the way to the bank – try laughing without vowels" (Maguire 1993: 60). Babel, babble, Babylon, language, languish, anguish.

5

PEERING INTO THE ABYSS: A POSTMODERN READING OF THE BIBLICAL BOTTOMLESS PIT[1]

Introduction: locating the abyss in the apocalyptic landscape

Consider a map of the Apocalypse of John. The geography of the text is broadly divided into the two spheres of heaven and earth. In heaven is the dwelling-place of God. On earth are the cities: of the seven churches, of Jerusalem (Mount Zion), and of Babylon. There are deserts, waters, and mountains. There are rural and urban areas and natural and supernatural realms.

Look around at the terrain of utopia: there is the New Jerusalem where God and the faithful dwell, but outside the city walls remain the active lake of fire and sulphur and the bottomless pit. There is a definite division of insider and outsider, and the focus of the textual map is split. After the great victory of God's army over evil, 'a holy city, the New Jerusalem' (Apoc. 21: 2) descends from heaven with new water and a tree of life (Apoc. 22: 1–5). The old earth with all its waters, dry land, and mighty cities is destroyed. Even Death and Hades are no more after they are thrown into the lake of fire (Apoc. 20: 13).

Is creation really new if chaos still abides outside the garden gates? Why does this gap, this rupture, this gaping hole remain in the textual landscape? Isn't God's future meant to be seamless and faultless, with all the evil powers and chaos destroyed for all time? Does the text throw the world back into an endless cycle of eternal return – out of chaos to creation and back again and again and again, never-ending? Is the textual map constantly deconstructing itself, falling into its own abyss?

Consider the following texts: "Death will be no more; mourning and crying and pain will be no more, for the first things have passed away" (Apoc. 21: 4). "Let the evildoer still do evil, and the filthy still be filthy, and the righteous still do right, and the holy still be holy" (Apoc. 22: 11). In other words, watch your step. The text is not ending neatly; rather, it is opening itself to the chaotic all over again.

As a postmodern reader of the Apocalypse I want to locate myself at the point on the textual map labeled ABYSS and enter the text from this place. The dot on the map is itself part of the rupture and is the site of an impossible location. The abyss is a place of difference – different from any other place. The abyss is a place that is totally "Other." To locate oneself at/in the pit means to be in a place that is no place, no ground, no bottom, no context.

The subject and the method of this chapter coincide. The abyss is a postmodern site because it is a site of conflict and struggle and chaos – the center that collapses. The abyss is an entry point into a strange and fragmented reading of the Apocalypse, a reading which is postmodern because it is not rooted in any historical-critical starting-point. A reading from the abyss is not "rooted" at all. In fact, to begin at the abyss is an "unnatural" starting-point. As Ihab Hassan defines postmodernism, "Indeterminacy elicits participation; gaps must be filled. The postmodern text, verbal or nonverbal, invites performance: it wants to be written, revised, answered, acted out" (1987: 10). The abyss represents what in postmodernism is the unrepresentable, the indeterminate, the fragmented, the self-less, and the depth-less.

The mythic place of the abyss on the textual map of the Apocalypse redefines space and location. The abyss is an imagined spot on the map – the impossible made possible in the fantasy of the end of time. The abyss is a dip in the landscape of the possible; it is the "jumping-off point" into nothingness. Its presence on the apocalyptic landscape is undeniable – and chilling. In the Apocalypse the abyss is a place of both warning and assurance for the believers. But even when assuring the believers of the safe-keeping of the evil powers in the abyss, there is always the possibility that the angel with the key will open the entrance door.

The abyss makes the landscape unstable. In their study of postmodern landscape, Trevor Barnes and James Duncan call attention to the development of landscape as a "social and cultural production":

Thus a landscape possesses a similar objective fixity to that of a written text. It also becomes detached from the intentions of its original authors, and in terms of social and psychological impact and material consequences the various readings of landscapes matter more than any authorial intentions. In addition, the landscape has an importance beyond the initial situation for which it was constructed, addressing a potentially wide range of readers.

(1992: 6)

Locating the abyss on the map of the Apocalypse is a particular way of reading and a way of entering the textual landscape. This gaping hole/pit is a starting-point, an ending-point, a bottomless point and thereby no point at all on the map. Reading for/at the abyss is a postmodern reading because it is a different positioning at the place of absolute difference (or *différance*, in the Derridean sense of both differ and defer). The abyss defers the closure of the text. There is no authorial control over the depths of this abysmal space. John measures the heavenly city, but the pit is measureless.

The map of the Apocalypse is a political map, for the destruction of the "world" (the Mediterranean basin) and its reconstruction as the political center of God's power in the New Jerusalem are all central.[2] In the margins are danger, evil, pollution, dishonor, exploding and endless disorder. The abyss is in the margins of the text. But there are no set boundaries. There is a door to heaven (Apoc. 4: 1) as there is on the pit (Apoc. 9: 1–2), but there is movement in and out of each domain. The reader is shown the pit in all its horror; if one is not marked on the forehead with the seal of God, the locusts that come out of the abysmal smoke will "torture them for five months, but not to kill them, and their torture was like the torture of a scorpion when it stings someone. And in those days people will seek death but will not find it they will long to die, but death will flee from them" (Apoc. 9: 5–6). This description of torture is good propaganda for becoming a servant of God!

Does the Apocalypse of John privilege order? Traditional readings of the text assert the final order of the end of time and God's victory over the forces of evil. I want to argue that this text is unbound in its own disorder – that the New Jerusalem as an ordered space is decentered by the well of chaos, which is seen as the abyss and the whole area outside the holy city where the evil powers dwell (in different states of punishment and tortured existence). The order is tenuous at best, with evil lurking outside the walls. The walls do not hold, they crumble, they "cave" in, so to speak. The city itself is on the edge of the abyss, and its ordered economy and demographics are constantly threatened. There is a prison for the evil beings and a lake of torture and death. The vision of a protective state is interrupted by the presence of horror, and horror is interrupted by the presence of the ordered state, and on and on.

The abyss as prison-house: defining its intertextual dimensions

In the Apocalypse of John the stories of destruction and creation swirl around the landscape. The supernatural and the natural collide and intersect. And this apocalyptic text collides with other biblical texts, other apocalyptic texts, readers, and the cultural values and manifestations of imagining the end of the world. Text and texts – text/s and worlds – interface. This basic definition of intertextuality as the relations of texts comes from Kristeva (1980, drawing from Bakhtin), Barthes (1977), and Derrida (1979). These textual relations and signification are often vague, problematic, warring, or with permeable boundaries. With the signifier a/b/y/s/s, the boundaries are broken through; in fact, there are no boundaries, since the abyss has no boundaries. To write about the abyss is to write about nothingness, space turned upon space, the ground knocked out of meaning. As Kristeva states about the abject, the abyss is "the place where meaning collapses" (1982: 2).

None the less, the abyss has had its own history of interpretation. The abyss is part of all the apocalyptic action; it is a prison-house[3] for evil monsters:

> Then I saw an angel coming down from heaven, holding in his hand the key to the bottomless pit and a great chain. He seized the dragon, that ancient serpent, who is the Devil and Satan, and bound him for a thousand years, and threw him into the pit, and locked and sealed it over him, so that he would deceive the nations no more, until the thousand years were ended. After that he must be let out for a little while.
>
> (Apoc. 20: 1–3)

Abyss, *abussos* in Greek, has many definitions. As seen from the passage above, the abyss is a spirit prison (from which the

Anti-Christ and his evil cohorts ascend). Even more basic, the abyss is a bottomless pit, a well, the deep (Hebrew *tehôm*), the interior of the earth, a place of exile, the original flood waters under the earth, chaos, the primordial goddess, the source of the universe, the underworld (but not the place of eternal punishment).[4] In Gnosticism the abyss is "the Supreme Being and the author of the Aeons" (Cooper 1978: 10). Christian mystics dwelt on the "creation out of nothing" aspect of the abyss; one descends into the abyss to experience the pure essence of God (McRay 1986: 18–19).

Although the abyss is not Sheol, Gehenna, or hell, the post-biblical tradition begins to merge these metaphors into an underworld place of eternal punishment. In some early Christian apocalypses, the abyss is more than a holding cell; it is also a torture chamber. The image of the mouth of hell develops during this period and is fully imagined in the medieval hell-mouth iconography of a beast's or bird's (owl's) mouth (see Davidson and Seiler 1992; Wickham 1987). One of the most graphic images of the abyss as hell mouth appears in the Apocalypse of Paul 32:

> The abyss has no measure; moreover there also follows on it the (gulf, void?) which is below it. And it is as if perhaps someone takes a stone and throws it into a very deep well and after many hours it reaches the ground; so is the abyss. For when these souls are thrown in they have scarcely reached the bottom after five hundred years.
>
> (Reddish 1990: 310)

This well in the Apocalypse of Paul is "sealed with seven seals." When Paul desires to look in the well, his guide angel says in Chapter 42:

> Open the mouth of the well that Paul, God's dearly beloved, may look in, because power has been given him to see all the punishments of the underworld. And the angel said to me: Stand at a distance, for you will not be able to bear the stench of this place. Then when the well was opened there came up immediately a disagreeable and very evil smell which surpassed all the punishments. And I looked into the well and saw fiery masses burning on all sides, and the narrowness of the well at its mouth was such that it was only able to take a single man.
>
> (Reddish 1990: 314–15)[5]

This hell mouth is a narrow passage which spews smoke and odors. Compare 1 Enoch 88: 1, "that abyss was narrow, and deep, and horrible and dark" (Reddish 1990: 45). But in Isaiah 5: 14 the mouth is opened wide: "Therefore Sheol has enlarged its appetite and opened its mouth beyond measure."[6]

The biblical deep is not just full of water; a large variety of sea monsters and serpents reside in the watery chaos. The basis for this view of the dangerous depths of the abyss is found in Psalm 42: 7: "Deep calls to deep at the thunder of your cataracts." In the Apocalypse of John the depths spit out smoke which contains locusts, which are monstrous winged figures on horses with human faces, women's hair, lion's teeth, and scorpion tales which sting and torture their victims (Apoc. 9: 3–10).[7] The beast which kills the two witnesses comes out of the abyss (Apoc. 11: 7). The abyss is the place of monsters and all sorts of impurities. Evil angels are the inmates of the abyss in 1 Enoch 21: 10: "This place (is) the prison of the angels, and there they will be held for ever" (Reddish 1990: 157). This text echoes 2 Peter 2: 4 in which the sinful angels are cast into Tartaros (hell) until Judgment Day. In Jude 6 the angels are bound in chains for safekeeping until their trial.

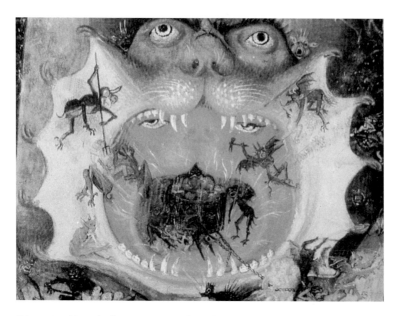

Figure 5.1 Detail of a hell mouth/abyss from the *Hours of Catherine of Cleves* (fifteenth century)

From the orifice of the pit come horrible bodily discharges. The Apocalypse of Peter 8 gives a particularly graphic image of the:

> very deep pit and into it there flow all kinds of things from everywhere: judgment (?) horrifying things and excretions. And the women (are) swallowed up (by this) up to their necks and are punished with great pain.... And the milk of the mothers flows from their breasts and congeals and smells foul, and from it come forth beasts that devour flesh...
>
> (Reddish 1990: 249–50)

The excretions and foul smells are part of the torture. Most of all, "there are wheels of fire, and men and women hung thereon by the power of their whirling. Those in the pit burn" (Apoc. Peter 12; Reddish 1990: 252; cf. 1 Enoch 90: 24–5).

The angel in charge of the abyss is identified in Apoc. 9: 1: "And the fifth angel blew his trumpet, and I saw a star that had fallen from heaven to earth, and he was given the key to the shaft of the bottomless pit" and more specifically in verse 11, "his name in Hebrew is Abaddon, and in Greek he is called Apollyon." Abaddon is the name of the destroyer angel and king of the underworld but is not Satan.[8] In Albrecht Dürer's 1498 woodcut, Abaddon/Apollyon is throwing the Dragon down the narrow entrance of the abyss (Apoc. 20: 1). The stories of the fallen angels from Gen. 6: 1–4 and 1 Enoch 6–8 tell of more than 200 angels falling to earth. Eventually, these fallen angels fall even further into the interior of the earth. Leonard Thompson points out that "the evil beasts in the Apocalypse (Apollyon; beast from the sea; scarlet beast) are variations on one another" (1990: 80). Evil monsters are difficult to tell apart, especially in the heat of the apocalyptic moment, with the beast in hot pursuit or disappearing into the bottomless pit into destruction – or rather, a limited prison sentence.

The abyss is imagined as a place of pain, or to borrow Robert Detweiler's phrase, as a "text of pain"[9] which describes texts which are written on the body (1989: 123). The abyss is both a part of the earth and a part of the body, the female sexual organs. As with Marduk's defeat of Tiamat in the *Enuma Elish*, the body of the mother goddess is divided into pieces, into a fragmented body; the male triumphs.[10] In the Apocalypse the female body is used to create the New City, and the triumphal males enter to live in this well-ordered place. All that remains outside the city are the "remains," the sexual center of the female. So does the male triumph completely and absolutely? Or does the presence of the abyss create such desire and terror because the ultimate Fall from grace, Eve's "sin," is (re)presented? As long as the abyss remains on the textual landscape, there is no certainty and no Truth. The text and the body are dismembered. The abyss is a body part laid bare and strewn throughout the text.

Is there a source to the abyss? Its concept of bottomlessness is an impossibility. In 1 Enoch 21: 7 the abyss is "full of great pillars of fire which were made to fall; neither its extent nor its size could I see, nor could I see its source" (Reddish 1990: 157). This concept of no origin relates to the Derridian idea that there is no source or origin to meaning, and it is a false direction to search for an origin. The abyss appears and disappears on the map. The abyss is the black hole in space; what happens when one is entered is still only speculation. Is the abyss where eroticism and death are linked? (Can this also be said of the New Jerusalem?) Could the bottomless pit be the ultimate joyride in the apocalyptic amusement park? Is its repeating presence for the reader's pleasure, always placing the reader on the brink of disaster? Or is the abyss the vanishing (or infinity) point on the canvas, with everything disappearing into a postmodern nihilism?

Approaching the mouth of the abyss is dangerous. The abyss is a cave, an endless serpent. Does this mouth have lips? Could this be the poison kiss – the kiss of death? Or are these "lips" the vulva? Does this mouth devour? Does this mouth have teeth – the *vagina dentata*, the agent of castration? Here is the prison-house of language, under lock and key. Usually words or sounds come out of a mouth; here there is only oral residue, the trace of the spoken, the trace of Wisdom, the hiss of signification.

Representing nothingness

The whole idea of chaos has been played out recently in the fields of science and literature. In science and mathematics chaos theory seeks to find the order out of disordered systems; the repeating systems are called "strange attractors," or patterns of order found in the deep structure of chaos. The unpredictable aspects of our world have a certain order to them; hidden inside the "random" changes in nature (e.g. natural disasters) is a pattern of order in the midst of chance. According to Antonio Benítez-Rojo in his study of Caribbean literature, "Chaos looks toward everything that repeats, reproduces, grows, decays, unfolds, flows, spins, vibrates, seethes" (1992: 3). Instead of filling the chaos of a text with an ordered or structured reading, post-structuralist and postmodernist readings allow for chaos to have precedence, to create its own space and disorder. In other words, meaning is indeterminant, and signifier and signified are unbound in an endless spiral.

This connection between chaos theory and postmodernism has best been made by Katherine Hayles. She investigates chaos theory, fractal geometry, the deconstructive theory of Jacques Derrida, Roland Barthes' reading of Sarrazine, and Michael Serres' philosophical interpretations. The main connection is that "both discourses invert traditional priorities: chaos is deemed to be more fecund than order, uncertainty is privileged above predictability, and fragmentation is seen as the reality that arbitrary definitions of closure would deny" (1990: 176). The rifts, holes, fissures, and ruptures of texts are the focal points of postmodernism. In discussing Derrida's *Of Grammatology*, Hayles notes that texts "are resevoirs of chaos" that are "always already" chaotic. Derrida's term is the concept of iteration, where a word has different meanings in different contexts (1990: 180). Iteration occurs in the "folds" of a text – textual spaces of repetition. "The fold can be thought of as a way to create the illusion of origin," Hayles adds, while iteration "unfolds" the text so that there is no point of origin (1990: 181). Hayes summarizes, "For deconstructionists, chaos repudiates order; for scientists, chaos makes order possible" (1990: 184).[11]

For Hayles, postmodernism constructs a "denaturing process" in which language, context, time, and the human are denatured (1990: 266). The new world created in the Apocalypse is a denatured world where nature and history collapse. The tree and waters of life in the New Jerusalem are repetitions of their Eden versions in Genesis. The origin of the world created out of the depths/chaos is repeated in the abyss, where there is no bottom, no origin. Perhaps there is a "future shock" (Alvin Toffler) where the future is used up before it happens (1990: 280),[12] and any human concept of time expands. John is a sort of time traveller who is able to break loose of his prison on Patmos to explore future worlds, while the horror of his present world is forever seeping into the future visions of hope and vice versa. There is no escaping chaos in the Apocalypse. Chaos is everywhere, past, present, and future.

Chaos represents Otherness (*différance*), and chaos like the abyss in the Apocalypse is a female concept. Hayles criticizes the chaos theorician James Gleick for his reification of male-based scientific knowledge and the ignoring of women scientists in his discussion of chaos. Hayles accuses Gleick of maintaining science as exclusively male, while "it is the particular project of this domain to have intercourse with a feminine principle" (1990: 174). Hayles further observes:

> But otherness is also always a threat, arousing the desire to control it, or even more extremely to subsume it within the known boundaries of the self, thus annihilating the very foreignness that makes it dangerously attractive.... The desire to control chaos is evident in the search for ways to rationalize it. By finding within it structures of order, these scientists have in effect subsumed chaos in the familiar. But if this incorporation were entirely successful, chaos could no longer function in its liberating role as a representation of the other.
>
> (1990: 173)

The otherness of the abyss in the Apocalypse represents the ultimate threat, the ultimate dangerous female. The abyss is the ruptured female, the ruptured hymen, no longer virgin, nor virgin mother, but the place of the vaginal birth of the universe. The evil women in the Apocalypse, Jezebel and the Whore of Babylon are clearly not virgins. The Woman Clothed with the Sun is a repeating of the Mary/Mother of God myth. The Bride of Christ is a virginal bride, but when she becomes the New Jerusalem she is entered by the believers and the company of God, including her husband, the Lamb. Still, the virginal women have maintained shame, which is represented by the hymen (see Malina 1981: 42–8). The abyss is yet another female character in the Apocalypse, representing the primordial female, chaos, the deep waters under the earth.

The presence of the abyss in the text seduces the reader. Like drivers who slow down to stare at an automobile accident, the gaze of the text on the monstrous and the horrible shows the pull of desire to look in that direction. There is a definite gaze on the female in the Apocalypse, and this gaze is controlling. The female is marked and sectioned off, and violence follows, either by death, exile, or the use of the body to create a new city. The abyss also receives this gaze. The abyss as female is Other, and the Other in the Apocalypse is feared and desired all at once. Demons enter the abyss, while only the purified people and spirits of God enter the Bride.

To return to the notion of the abyss as the female organ, as vagina and ruptured hymen – what is also present in this line of thinking is what the abyss is *not*, or what it lacks, which is the phallus. Following a Freudian line, the abyss represents castrated woman/mother. The female must hide her shame, her lack. According to Jacques Lacan, "the phallus can play its role only when veiled" (1977: 288).[13] Elizabeth Grosz comments on this Lacanian concept of veiling:

> This gap or lack is also the founding trace of the unconscious, constituted as such by the repressed signifier: "It is the ultimately significative object which appears when all the veils are lifted. Everything related to it is an object of amputations and interdictions…. When the veils are lifted, there is only the Medusa[14] – women's castrated genitals, lacking, incomplete, horrifying (for men). Salomé's dance, like strip-tease, can only seduce when at least one veil remains, alluring yet hiding the *nothing* of woman's sex.
>
> (1990:121)

Is the sealing door to the abyss a type of veil? For Kristeva, that which horrifies, the abject, is veiled: "The time of abjection is double: a time of oblivion and thunder, of veiled infinity and the moment when revelation bursts forth" (1982: 9). So, too, for Derrida: "Truth, unveiling, illumination are no longer decided in the appropriation of the truth of being, but are cast into its bottomless abyss as non-truth, veiling and dissimulation…" (1979: 119). The door to the abyss is a locked and sometimes lifted veil.

The abyss represents both the Unconscious and unconscious desires. Only the angel has the key (on "a great chain"!) with which he can unlock the covering over the mouth. This focus on lack and on castration is a phallocentric way of imagining the abyss. Grosz follows Irigarary's definition of phallocentrism as the centering of the male as normative for human behavior. She states:

> As the sexual other to the One sex, woman has only been able to speak or to be heard as an undertone, a murmur, a rupture within discourse; or else she finds her expression in a hysterical fury, where the body "speaks" a discourse that cannot be verbalized by her.
>
> (1990: 174)

As a "rupture within discourse" the abyss is a hysterical place, when the veil or lid is taken off. Or is it a place of *jouissance*? God places an angel guard in control of the entrance/mouth of the abyss. Only the mouth is bound and maintained. But the rupture is deep, so that there is no end to chaos (or revelation) in the "end."

The rupture is not the rupture caused by castration (or clitoridectomy), but rather caused by (sexual experience) and the birthing process. Still, the abyss represents chaos and must be controlled under lock and key.[15] What remains is the murmur, the rupture the presence of the abyss places in the text. The abyss remains a gendered space, a female space.

Conclusion: trangressing boundaries

Who will descend into the abyss?

(Romans 10: 7)

The apocalyptic abyss is part of the Western cultural landscape.[16] In literary, theological, and philosophical traditions, the fascination with the abyss has taken the imagination into new realms of the supernatural underworld – in particular, into one realm that is a more ordered chaos, that of hell. Eventually, the concept of hell developed into a hierarchically structured place, in direct opposition to the hierarchy of heaven. But the abyss remained in the margins of the apocalyptic imagination as the true chaos, with no order, no form, no plot, no characters, no narrator, etc. The abyss crosses all boundaries; it is boundless. How does something that ruptures all form fit into an apocalyptic vision of how God is going to re-form the world?

The visions of the Apocalypse of John are of a world with an imposed order. The mouth of the abyss is guarded and only opened under divine command. There is a pre-designed plan for the boundaries of the New World. This aspect of fixity in Christianity is critiqued by philosopher Georges Bataille:

> The Christian God is a highly organised and individual entity springing from the most destructive of feelings, that of continuity. Continuity is reached when boundaries are crossed. But the most constant characteristic of the impulse I have called transgression is to make order out of what is essentially chaos. By introducing transcendence into an

organised world, transgression becomes a principle of an organised disorder.

(1986: 119)

The presence of the abyss in the text makes all boundaries useless. Continuity disintegrates when the mouth of the abyss is transgressed. The original chaos survives with all its depths intact. The philosophical roots of a postmodern reading of the abyss come from Friedrich Nietzsche's question, "Is seeing itself – not seeing abysses?" (1961: 177, quoted in Watson 1985: 245), which reflects the nihilism resulting from any attempt to ground knowledge in God. Nietzsche is responding to the Kantian idea of "*der Wahre Ab-grund*," which translates as " ...true abyss. The truth of grounding, to be *without* grounds" (Watson 1985: 229). This loss of ground is the loss of truth and knowledge. In other words, there are some things that cannot be known completely, despite science and reason, and this groundlessness is the problem of abysses, for philosophers such as Kant, Hegel, Heidegger, Nietzsche, and Derrida. Stephen Watson summarizes the line of philosophical thinking about the abyss back to the essence of God (a focus of the medieval mystics); deconstructionists (following Nietzsche) say that this essence or origin is the abyss; still the abyss is continually problematized. The abyss is a problem in philosophical thought because it represents infinity, the endless repetition of time, being, and knowledge that is never fixed or rooted or rational.

The abyss is what one sees when one sees the Other. Watson understands the Nietzschean abyss as affirming difference:

> There is a refusal to reduce all attributes to an univocity. A refusal, therefore, of ontology, of "Being," all is interpretation and exegesis. The world is, in short, an abyss, and *Ab-grund*.... It is a chasm of infinite alterity, the infinite return of this Other with a Same. It is the return of the Other, of becoming, of difference.
>
> (1985: 233)

When the abyss is faced, the Other is faced. Perhaps the abyss should be written abyss, crossed through to point to the non-origin, the absence the abyss represents.[17] This Other of the abyss in the Apocalypse is the abject (Kristeva: 1982) – that which is horrible and profane. In the abyss are linked Female-Other-Death, the trinity of the sacrificial mode. The body of the female is sacrificed throughout the Apocalypse, but with the abyss is left a body part, a chasm which devours horrors and spews forth some of the most horrible evil beasts imaginable. The interior of the abyss is not described; it is too horrible to imagine. So the text stops at the mouth, and the opening is perhaps the scariest part of all.

The desire for primordial creation, the big birth, repeats itself in the apocalyptic narrative. The abyss is the creative power of the female. The boundaries of the dualism of male/female, culture/nature, and mind/body are disrupted. The whole text is left in ruins. The boundaries of the New Jerusalem seem impenetrable, but they are not a stable entity in the text, for this future city is always not yet. The abyss is always already.

The abyss is the excess of desire, surplus erotic power. The focus at the end of the twentieth century is on human power to destroy the world through nuclear and/or environmental holocaust. In the Apocalypse of John the focus is on God's power to destroy the world. Of course, Christian fundamentalists still hold diligently to this theology.[18] They have a fascination with the horror of the end time; they stand close to the edge of the abyss, straining to peer in as Paul did in the Apocalypse of Paul. Current historical events in the Middle East are read with anticipation of the soon-to-come horrors. The evil beast is soon to be spat out of the hell mouth.

In the abyss "all is interpretation and exegesis," and there is no end to this process. So to say that in the Apocalypse of John the abyss means such-and-such is ultimately to say nothing. Historical-critical exegesis desires a grounding in meaning which is no ground. The Apocalypse is not a history book of the late twentieth or the late first century. The exegete is left with no place to stand, for to stand in the abyss is to stand in no place.

The end of the Bible returns to the beginning. There is an echo or trace of the nothingness, the formless void, from the beginning. There is the possibility of a new and different creation, another text. Leaving the void intact creates the possibility of change. Maybe this time the story will be different.

6

APOCALYPTIC HORROR[1]

Descend into a tale of darkness. Enter a world, a mirror-world of your own earth, but one in which supernatural beings fill every space. Monsters roam, freedom dissolves, and death and destruction are at every turn. The violence is overwhelming. There is no escape. You are soaked in blood – your own? another's? a monster's? You are surrounded by spirits, the dead, fire, plagues, war, and natural disasters. Imagine the worst; imagine the end of time, the last days of earth. Every place on earth is burning and nothing and no one survives on the old earth. You experience the ultimate holocaust.

> It is useless to hope: things are there; born or stillborn, they are there, done.... The heavens have come down to earth. We sense the fatal taste of material paradise. It drives one to despair, but what should one do? *No future*....
>
> Everything has already been wiped off the map. It is useless to dream: the *clash* has gently taken place everywhere.... Look around: this explosion has already occurred.
>
> (Baudrillard 1989: 34)

The last book of the New Testament tells this tale of horror. The Apocalypse of John, a late first century CE text of the end times, creates a scenario of God's final judgment of humanity. Apocalypse is a revelation (in Greek, *apokalyptein*, to uncover, take the lid/veil off), a revealing of and a revelling in (see Quinby 1994: xiii) the end time horrors. The narrator is John of Patmos; a series of heavenly angels guide John through the visions. John guides the reader in the proper responses to these visions: fall down in utter fear as though dead (1: 17). Be terrified, for the Apocalypse is a text of terror.

The Apocalypse is a tale of horror and of the excess of desire for the violent end time events. As horror tale, the excess of the Apocalypse leaks off its biblical pages into a Western cultural context of millennial visions of God's final judgment. What does the literature of horror – from Gothic romances to contemporary shudder pulps – have to do with a biblical text? What do horror theory and fictions (literature, movies, art) have to offer in reading the Apocalypse of John? As Kirk Schneider relates, "Even in ancient times, biblical writers understood our enchantment with the macabre" (1993: xi). I want to take my previous work on the Apocalypse and the fantastic a step further, a step beyond. Is the Apocalypse cathartic? What is the fascination with a story of such intense violence? And why are apocalyptic visions like Hal Lindsey's *The Late Great Planet Earth* and Stephen King's *The Stand* so popular? Why do we need to imagine and experience the end time horrors before they occur? Why express our worse fears (and hopes?) in literary form so we can share our anxieties with others? Horror theory is useful in examining the emotional aspects of apocalyptic fiction and those leaks into the cultural narrative.

Horrality theory

> The horror film is an invitation to indulge in deviant, anti-social behavior by proxy – to commit gratuitous acts of violence, indulge our puerile dreams of power, to give in to our most craven fears.
>
> (Stephen King 1983: 31)

> Yes, folks, in *The Stand* I got a chance to scrub the whole human race, and *it was fun*!
>
> (Stephen King 1983: 402)

The many horrors of the Apocalypse of John draw on the power of the prophetic vision of future events. What is impossible in real life – the destruction of the colonizing government and all that is evil in the world – is possible in the realm of the horror fantasy. Present fears and oppressions are visible in the vivid descriptions of the monstrous and its destruction. The invisible supernatural forces and spirits are visible in the Apocalypse. Everything that is alien is invited to this horror show. The evil powers are in plain view now.

The prophetic vision of horror also has an aspect of hope. "Good" defeats "evil" in the end. But the Apocalypse's narrative of the supernatural victory of good over evil has an uncanny edge. The uncanny has several meanings, beginning with Freud's definition of *das Unheimliche*, a mixture of the familiar and the strange. Freud's base definition of the uncanny is that it "is undoubtedly related to what is frightening – to what arouses dread and horror… it tends to coincide with what excites fear in general" (1958: 219). When one experiences the familiar in unfamiliar and dangerous ways, the uncanny is present. Rosemary Jackson observes that *das Unheimliche* "functions to dis-cover, reveal, expose areas normally kept out of sight. It uncovers what is hidden and, by doing so, effects a disturbing transformation of the familiar into the unfamiliar" (1981: 65).[2] In discussing Cixous on the uncanny, Jackson states, "The uncanny… removes structure…. Cixous presents its unfamiliarity not as merely displaced sexual anxiety, but as a rehearsal of an encounter with death, which is pure absence" (1981: 68). This discovering and revelation in the uncanny is what "apocalypse" is all about. What is concealed is desire – desire for death (of the enemy and ourselves?) and the final judgment and the war to end all wars. Is the uncanny in apocalyptic discourse a desire for what we desire most or least?

In terms of Todorov's (1973) structuralist model for the fantastic, horror literature has elements of the uncanny (connected with natural and psychological explanations) but also of the marvelous (grounded in belief in the supernatural and the magical). Horror literature does not fit easily into one of these structuralist categories of the marvelous, fantastic-marvelous, fantastic-uncanny, or uncanny. Noël Carroll states,

> Even if horror belongs to the genus of the fantastic-marvelous, it constitutes a distinctive species…. For horror appears to be one of those genres in which the emotive responses of the audience, ideally, run parallel to the emotions of characters. Indeed, in works of horror the responses of characters often seem to cue the emotional responses of the audiences.
>
> (1990: 17, cf. 150)

Many literalistic readings of the Apocalypse attempt to give contemporary explanations for the mythic creatures and happenings and to involve the reader directly in the events. For example, Hal Lindsey (1980) seems to say, "Hey, this really is happening to us in the late twentieth century and here's exactly how it translates and how it will all work out for the believer and unbeliever." Todorov stresses the necessity of hesitation and ambiguity on the part of the reader of fantasy, and with horror literature fear accompanies this hesitation (1973: 33).[3] Literalistic expositions play on this fear component by adding to and enhancing and exaggerating the horrors of the Apocalypse. John's vision is occurring now, and there is no way to stop the horror. The explosion has already occurred; the monsters have been set loose on the world.

Even for readers not very familiar with the details of the plot of the Apocalypse, the basic idea of its weird supernatural vision of the end is well known. The seer John of Patmos receives a series of visions in which the angel army of God defeats the evil beasts and politicos of the earth and all unbelievers in God. In the opening verses the narrator explains the divine transmission:

> The revelation of Jesus Christ which God gave him to show his servants what must soon take place; he made it known by sending his angel to his servant John, who testified to the word of God and to the testimony of Jesus Christ, even to all that he saw. Blessed is the one who reads aloud the words of the prophecy, and blessed are those who hear and who keep what is written in it; for the time is near.
>
> (Apoc. 1: 1–3)

The mood is one of tense anticipation, for since the visions have been seen by John, each telling/hearing makes the end that much more imminent. The reader has divine permission to gaze on the horror. The Apocalypse is no cheap thrill. The end of the world as described by God is serious business.

This business of last things disturbs business-as-usual. The horrible intrudes into ordinary life; in the Apocalypse, political, economical (trade and agriculture), and human life come to a screeching halt. I use the word screeching because the Apocalypse is a loud narrative: loud voices from heaven (e.g. 1: 10; 6: 1; shouting in 10: 3); blaring trumpets (8: 6–11; 19); thunder (10: 3); mass wailing (5: 4; 18: 9, 11, 15, 18–19); singing (4: 8, 11; 5: 9–10, 12, 13; 7: 10, 12; 11: 15, 17–18; 15: 3–4). Only at 8: 1 is there silence: "When the Lamb opened the seventh seal, there was silence in heaven for about half an hour." Angels come and go, speaking all sorts of horror about the death and destruction. The narrative moves quickly through its series of sevens. Adela Yarbro Collins offers a general outline:

(1984: 112)

The scenes of heavenly worship intrude in the visions of earthly destruction. The narrator John takes the reader back and forth between the two realms. John looks at the heavenly activities from the earth: "After this I looked, and there in heaven a door stood open!" (4: 1). The angels, dragons, and deities travel back and forth between heaven and earth. John travels great distances on earth: "And in the spirit he carried me away to a great, high mountain and showed me the holy city Jerusalem coming down out of heaven from God" (21: 10). The effect of this realm-hopping is to show that each realm is terrifying, with strange creatures (like the elders and the four living creatures in heaven). Even the vision of the New Jerusalem is disconcerting. As Schneider relates, "Even so-called elated states of consciousness can become harrowing. Heaven, Paradise, Nirvana – all of these *sound* beautiful. But what might they *actually* be like? How do *eternal* submission or *unceasing* harmony strike us? What about *perpetual* enthusiasm?" (1993: 6). Or as Gunter Gebauer states, "Our imagination remains captive in the cave... all our notions of paradise are linked with situations of the cave" (1989: 28). Horror is entering the cave. Horror is about knowing the unknown and facing the deepest terrors. The repetition of horrors in series of sevens in the Apocalypse is a hard-hitting and constant jolt; the heavenly interludes are no rest, not even at the conclusion of the visions, for here also the unfamiliar dwells, with full, fantastic power over humans and the earth.

Why compare the Apocalypse to horror literature? In horror the unexpected happens. The dead come back to life, the supernatural acts in and on the world, and evil runs rampant (for a while and more). Human fear is central. Carroll offers a definition: "The word 'horror' derives from the Latin 'horrere' – to stand on end (as hair standing on end) or to bristle – and the old French 'orror' – to bristle or to shudder" (1990: 24). The path to paradise has dead bodies, evil monsters, heavenly messengers, heavenly throne room and altar, a magical scroll, a bottomless pit, fire, natural disasters, ecocide, sacrifice, rape, cannibalism, plagues, and uncertainty. There is a bloodbath on the way. Any one of these is enough to make one's hair stand on end. Everything is presented in extremes and is "larger than life." This supernatural spectacle captures the imagination; the horror of the Apocalypse creeps in, for the end of the world is the ultimate horror.

The Apocalypse is less like the shower scene in *Psycho* than the all-out killing in the *Texas Chain Saw Massacre*, but there are elements of both these forms of subtle and big screen gross-out horrors in the text. Apocalypse 14: 19–20 describes some of the terror: "So the angel swung his sickle over the earth and gathered the vintage of the earth, and he threw it into the great wine press of the wrath of God. And the wine press was trodden outside the city, and blood flowed from the wine press, as high as a horse's bridle, for a distance of about two hundred miles." Again at the murder scene of the Whore of Babylon in 17: 16 is grotesque terror: "And the ten horns that you saw, they and the beast will hate the whore; they will make her desolate and naked; they will devour her flesh and burn her up with fire." And the birds of midheaven feast on the flesh of kings and other leaders in "the great supper of God" (19: 17–18), "and all the birds were gorged with their flesh" (19: 21). The Apocalypse has similarities to the genre of horror literature in the splattering of blood and gore on the reader and in the intensity in which it draws the reader to gaze on the ripped flesh. What is the usual response to such scenes of violence? Because this text is sacred scripture to Christians are we taught to ignore the violence and to repress our revulsion?

Yet wading through the blood of the Apocalypse brings one to the heavenly city, which is the most bejewelled city imaginable, and according to most biblical scholarship the place of eternal comfort: "And I saw the holy, city, the new Jerusalem, coming down out of heaven from God, prepared as a bride adorned for her husband" (21: 2), and "It has the glory of God and a radiance like a very rare jewel, like jasper, clear as crystal" (21: 11). The city is eternal and infinite in its pleasures. Jacques Barazun comments on the infinite and transcendent nature of horror: "There we have it: the imagination is a window open on the infinite; and the sublime visions that we may find associated with it give us the delightful shudder of horror" (1986: 356). There is an unease in the New Jerusalem scene in the Apocalypse; the extreme purity is marked off only by a wall while, "Outside are the dogs and sorcerers and fornicators and murderers and idolaters, and everyone who loves and practices falsehood" (22: 15). The robes of the pure, the righteous, in the city have been washed in blood.

The natural and supernatural elements of the Apocalypse are similar to what is called "sublime horror." Broadly speaking, the idea of the sublime comes first from Longinus's Greek work, *On the Sublime*, to Edmund Burke and then Immanuel Kant.[4] The basic definition of the sublime is as "the element of Grandeur that inspires pleasurable awe in an observer" (Sullivan 1986: 409). Burke's idea of the sublime in literature was that the reader must maintain a certain safe distance from the object of fear in order to get the thrill of pleasure from it. In his *Critique of Judgment*, Kant has two kinds of sublime, the mathematical (dealing with the infinite) and the dynamical (as in natural wonders, like hurricanes). Kant explains the emotive response to the sublime:

> Thus any spectator who beholds massive mountains climbing skyward... and so on is indeed seized by *amazement* bordering on terror, by horror and a sacred thrill; but, since he knows he is safe, this is not actual fear: it is merely our attempt to incur it with our imagination, in order that we may feel that very power's might and connect the mental agitation this arouses with the mind's state of rest.
>
> (1987: 129)

Kant is speaking more of the fear that accompanies experiences with the transcendent than that which attends the revulsion associated with the horror genre from the Gothic to the contemporary slasher film. The aesthetic pleasure of the sublime is not found in emotive response to objects of disgust but in responses to nature and the transcendent God. Kant agrees with the narrator John of the Apocalypse that the appropriate response to God is prostration in worship, and this response must be morally grounded in reason. But he adds, "Only if he is conscious that his attitude is sincere and pleasing to God, will these effects of might serve to arouse in him the idea of God's sublimity..." (1987: 123). The aesthetics of horror is about this mixture of fear and pleasure when faced with the sublime. Although several horror theorists dismiss any connection between the sublime and contemporary art-horror,[5] the notion of the sublime does provide a foundational understanding of emotional responses to what is awesome and infinite.

Furthermore, Julia Kristeva focuses on the emotive elements of horror, or to use her term, the abject. "The abject is edged with the sublime," states Kristeva (1982: 11). "The time of abjection is double: a time of oblivion and thunder, of veiled infinity and the moment when revelation bursts forth" (1982: 9). Drawing from Mary Douglas's *Purity and Danger*, Kristeva bases her concept of abjection on the notion of that which is dangerous, taboo, outside, Other, i.e. the feminine.[6] The abject is both horrible and pleasurable (the concept of *jouissance*); in the abject, repressed phobias rise to the surface. Kristeva notes that the literature of abjection:

> represents the ultimate coding of our crises, of our most intimate and most serious apocalypses... literature may also involve not an ultimate resistance to but an unveiling of the abject: an elaboration, a discharge, and a hollowing out of abjection through the Crisis of the Word.
>
> (1982: 208)

In her metaphysical elaboration on the powers of horror Kristeva finds the abject in the law, prophetic literature, and the gospels, but the ultimate abjection is in the fiction of the end of the world, the Apocalypse. She quotes Céline: "All the great monstrosities, all of them are in Saint John!" (1982: 207). Fear, terror, revulsion, pleasure – the crisis of religion – of an all-powerful deity wreaking havoc on the universe and how to respond to this action intellectually and on a gut level – is encoded in the Apocalypse. When forced to face the ultimate horror, the response is to hide one's face: John falls down on his face to worship the Son of Man and God, but he is repeatedly told to stand and face the deity. Those who try to hide cannot:

> The sky vanished like a scroll rolling itself up, and every mountain and island was removed from its place. Then the kings of the earth and the magnates and the generals and the rich and the powerful, and everyone, slave and free, hid in the caves and among the rocks of the mountains, calling to the mountains and rocks, "Fall on us and hide us from

the face of the one seated on the throne and from the wrath
of the Lamb; for the great day of their wrath has come, and
who is able to stand?"

(Apoc. 6: 14–17)

One must face the horror, because a moral decision must be
made, and the choice is written on the foreheads: the mark of the
Beast (13: 16) or the mark of the Lamb (22: 4). Facing the horror is
part of the pleasurable torment of reading the Apocalypse.

In the Apocalypse desire is linked with horror; there is a certain
joyous response to the destruction and gory details (e.g. Handel's
Messiah). In general the emotional reactions to the Apocalypse may
include: disgust, uneasiness, revulsion, attraction, anxiety, fear,
terror, fascination, dread, excitement, confusion, guilt, gross-out, and
joy.[7] The narrator is fixated and obsessed with the details of the
horrible events. The world has never known such violence and terror.
The flooding of the earth in Genesis brought quick death to all but
the lucky few on the ark. But was God's promise, "nor will I ever
again destroy every living creature as I have done" (Gen. 8: 21), i.e.
through flooding, meant to put humanity at ease? Is the "no flood"
decision good news? And is the destruction of the earth and re-
creation of the heavenly realm on the earth something about which to
break into an "hallelujah chorus"? Is Handel's joyous rendering of the
Apocalypse just a little twisted, like the Apocalypse itself, inviting
us to dance joyously on the grave of the earth?[8]

One of the major issues of emotions and horror literature is
whether or not the range of emotions is coming from some
repressed desires of the reader. Freud would certainly say that
responses to the uncanny originate from repressed sexual desires
that are brought to the surface. Kristeva pushes the repression
theory to center on disgust and hatred of the female (body) as Other.
Historically based studies of the Apocalypse posit a theory of
catharsis; that is, the Apocalypse is a cathartic narrative for both
ancient and modern reader, since the narrative provides an
emotional release in a world of trauma. Yarbro Collins notes, "As
expressive language, the book of Revelation creates a virtual experience for the hearer or reader" (1984: 144). For her, the "virtual
experience" is that the hearer/reader confronts God's power and
human powerlessness, but God's power is certain enough to bring
relief in the face of trauma (1984: 152). She states further, "Feelings
of fear and resentment are released by the book's repeated presentations of the destruction of the hearers' enemies" (1984: 154). Yarbro

Collins sees the Apocalypse operating as a vehicle for the release of fear. She acknowledges the intensity of fear in the text, and this fear is defeated as God defeats the powers of evil. The cathartic effect of the Apocalypse helps the reader face the fear of martyrdom. But this cathartic explanation is limited.[9] The fear raised by the horror of the text is not completely expelled at the end: "Do not seal up the words of the prophecy of this book, for the time is near. Let the evil-doer still do evil, and the filthy still be filthy, and the righteous still do right, and the holy still be holy" (Apoc. 22: 10–11). Moreover, the end of the world is still and always imminent. Todorov's concept of hesitation on the part of the reader relates here. The repeated expectation of the end of the world repeats the horror in each reading. Dieter Lenzen calls this repetition a disease, "apocalypsia," "making sense of the situation by threatening an apocalypse and preventing the end of the world by symbolically simulating it" (1989: 75). He adds, "nobody is really frightened that the world is coming to an end, but a life without anxiety is much too dangerous" (1989: 75). The expansiveness of horror includes the need to enact the end of the world again and again. The glory of the intrusion of paradise on earth remains unsettling. The mysterious, supernatural deity wins the battle each time. So are we to breathe a sigh of relief, of fear released?

Imagining monsters

> Monstrosity always reveals a truth.
>
> (Huet 1993: 128)

The power of horror in the Apocalypse is embodied in its monsters. Consider the description of the beast of the sea:

> I saw a beast rising out of the sea; and on its horn were ten diadems, and on its heads were blasphemous names. And the beast I saw was like a leopard, its feet were like a bear's, and its mouth was like a lion's mouth. And the dragon gave it his power and his throne and great authority. One of its heads seemed to have received a death-blow, but its mortal wound had been healed. In amazement the whole earth followed the beast.... "Who is like the beast, and who can fight against it?"
>
> (Apoc. 13: 1–4)

The power of the monstrous image stands out in every scene of the Apocalypse, whether it be a beast (great red dragon or land or sea beast), Satan, the false prophet, an evil animal creature (locusts in 9: 3 and "foul spirits like frogs" in 16: 13), the abyss, the birds of midheaven that devour human flesh, the four horsemen, the Jezebel, the Whore of Babylon, the enemy cavalry, Death and Hades – or – the twenty-four elders, the four living creatures, the 144,000, the Woman Clothed with the Sun, the earth/goddess Gaia who swallows the red dragon's vomit flood, the Bride of Christ, the Spirit, the two witnesses, martyrs under the altar, the angel Michael and his heavenly angel armies, and yes, the Lamb, the Son of Man, even to God on the throne.[10] All these images are supernatural and horrifying in different ways. The description of the Son of Man elucidates this point of the extremity of monstrous in the Apocalypse:

> and in the midst of the lampstands I saw one like the Son of Man, clothed with a long robe and with a golden sash across his chest. His head and his hair were white as white wool, white as snow; his eyes were like a flame of fire, his feet were like burnished bronze, refined as in a furnace, and his voice was like the sound of many waters. In his right hand he held seven stars, and from his mouth came a sharp, two-edged sword, and his face was like the sun shining with full force.
>
> When I saw him, I fell at his feet as though dead.
>
> (Apoc. 1: 13–17)

Of the two lengthy descriptions above, which is more terrifying? The power of each image induces terror. Mythic figures represent both evil and good, and both have magical powers over humans. Who or what is a monster? The Apocalypse has us look up close. Horrific details are given. Monsters are freakish; monsters devour; monsters want to control our lives by tricking us with falsehood. Ancient readers were asked/forced to imagine political figures as beasts – colonialism as alien and as an alien invasion.

The monsters of the Apocalypse are of a different species, an animal-human-mineral configuration. Carroll calls this composition "fusion" (1990: 43), and a clear example is in Apocalypse 9: 7–10:

> In appearance the locusts were like horses equipped for battle. On their heads were what looked like crowns of

gold; their faces were like human faces, their hair like women's hair, and their teeth like lions' teeth; they had scales like iron breastplates, and the noise of their wings was like the noise of many chariots with horses rushing into battle. They have tails like scorpions, with stingers, and in their tails is their power to harm people for five months.

Carroll defines horrific monsters as "threatening," "impure," "dangerous," and "lethal." But a monster may also be "threatening psychologically, morally, or socially. It may destroy one's identity," "seek to destroy the moral order," "or advance an alternative society" (1990: 43). He further summarizes: "That is, monsters are native to places outside of and/or unknown to the human world. Or the creatures come from marginal, hidden, or abandoned sites… they belong to environs outside of and unknown to ordinary social intercourse" (1990: 35). Although the Lamb and Son of Man creatures that represent Jesus Christ are pure and "good," as opposed to the evil, impure beasts, I want to argue that they, along with all the heavenly creatures, are also terrifying monsters.

The Son of Man and the Lamb are described, but only those admitted into the heavenly city will see the face of God (Apoc. 22: 4); otherwise God remains a mysterious father (14: 1) figure seated on the throne and known only as a right hand (5: 1 with a scroll), a voice, and a breath (spirit, 11: 11). But God is not a disembodied voice in the Apocalypse; pieces of God are revealed with the promise of full disclosure to come for the lucky faithful few. The mystery adds to the sense of awesomeness of the divine. The throne is often mentioned and is metonymic for God. God is a divine ruler, and God's successor is "a male child, who is to rule all the nations with a rod of iron" (12: 5), a truly comforting thought!

As with the many types of monsters in the Apocalypse, the central body part is the mouth: the voice of God and the angels and the Son of Man with the "sharp, two-edged sword" in his mouth (cf. 19: 13–14). The rider in Apocalypse 19: 21 also has a sword coming out of his mouth. The red dragon tries to devour the messianic child (12: 4) and send a flood on the child's mother from his mouth (12: 15). God spits/vomits the lukewarm water of the church at Laodicea (3: 16), and Gaia "opened its mouth and swallowed the river the dragon had poured from his mouth" (12: 16). The locusts have lion's teeth (9: 8), and the beast from the sea has a lion's mouth (13: 2) out of which he blasphemes: "The beast was given a mouth

Figure 6.1 Whore of Babylon in plastic snow (glitter) bubble with the three crosses of Calvary in the background. (Bought in a novelty shop in San Francisco, 1997.)

Source: Photo by the author.

uttering haughty and blasphemous words" (13: 5 and 15). Evil spirits like frogs come out "from the mouth of the dragon, from the mouth of the beast, and from the mouth of the false prophet" (16: 13). The ten horns and the beast devour the Whore (cannibalism in 17: 16) who has drunk the blood of the saints and martyrs (17: 6). The most terrifying mouth of all is the mouth of the abyss. Clive Barker notes that horror is "stories of the body," and these stories are about "our confrontation as spirits with the brutal business of phys-icality" (quoted in Carroll 1990: 239). The point is that all these images are terrifying, but one wants to be on the winning side.

The evil beasts are all thrown into the lake of fire or imprisoned in the bottomless pit, but of course they all deserve this punishment and destruction. Originally, all the supernatural creatures are in heaven together, until war breaks out and the dragon and his angel company are thrown out by God's angel armies (12: 7–9). There is a funeral dirge for the Whore of Babylon ("Fallen, fallen" in 18: 2) and a burial service for the beast and the false prophet who are "thrown alive into the lake of fire that burns with sulfur" (19: 20). Death and Hades and all impure evildoers are also thrown in the lake of fire (20: 14–15; 21: 8). All their torturing of humans is outdone in the final judgment. The cross is not the last instrument of torture; God invents more cruel forms of imprisonment and death. Immense pain is inflicted; the earth at the end during the "tribulation" becomes a torture chamber. Schlobin rightly observes that we see the destruction "through the monster's eyes" (1992: 29); we take the position of the monster when the victim is destroyed. There are many monsters in the Apocalypse, but the real bad ass monster sits on the heavenly throne.

In horror literature the unexpected happens – the dead come back to life, angels exist and speak, and evil is thoroughly (?) destroyed. How do we define evil? As death, destruction, torture, genocide, gynocide, the complete holocaust of the end of the world? The monster committing these deeds is not the as/sorted beasts who "represent" (and embody) evil. Who is responsible for this final holocaust? God/Son of Man/Lamb does more evil (for good?) than any other monster in the text. The beasts are certainly cruel, but the destructive God of the Apocalypse is far more cruel.[11] The familiar all-loving and compassionate deity is set against the unfamiliar image of a cruel deity. The apocalyptic God is not impotent or sterile; he fathers a child in Chapter 12 – is this a monstrous birth?[12] Is the Son (of Man, sword in mouth) the spitting image of

Figure 6.2 Celestial Season's Tension Tamer Tea – photograph on packaging
Source: Photo by the author.

the Father? The wrath of God is in full force in the Apocalypse (e.g. 11: 18; 14: 10, 19; 15: 1, 7; 16: 1, 19; 19: 15). God's wrath fills bowls and cups and wine presses. Is the Apocalypse telling a story of a just God? Is the Apocalypse a story of justice? What Schlobin says about the Book of Job holds true for the Apocalypse: "If anything, the moral is that there is no certainty from the divine. Everything can be taken away and maimed for nothing more than a wager" (1992: 34).[13] In other words, God is a monster who can always return, always enact wrath. And there is much more at stake in the enactment of the end of the world. The world is not saved but destroyed and replaced. God is a destroyer, the leader of the ultimate massacre.[14] Although in the Apocalypse the promises for the faithful witnesses are great, the vengeful deity is incredibly frightening.

Pornoapocalypse

> ...the secret of Paradise: it was the kingdom of *perversity*.
> (Žižek 1997: 15)

Žižek's "the seven veils of fantasy" (1997), like the (in)famous dance of the seven veils of the sacred prostitute, invite the gaze. Variants of the Greek word *porneia* appear in the Apocalypse and stand for "unrestricted sexual indulgence" (Hauck and Schulz 1968: 594). Jezebel and her followers are accused of this indulgence, as are the Whore and her followers. Both female figures are stripped in this accusation – Jezebel is thrown on a bed and the Whore is stripped naked. The Greek root *apokalyptein* means to reveal, expose, uncover – is something pornographic revealed? Does the Apocalypse consist of highly eroticized visions of extreme violence? Consider Lovis Corinth's 1916 lithograph *The Whore of Babylon*. The beautiful, smiling Whore lies on her side as the ten horns and the beast, along with the kings of the earth, devour her (Apoc. 17: 16). All who gaze on her are amazed. Peter Brooks describes such scenes as that of "viewing woman's body in a phallic field of vision" (1993: 199). The exotic/erotic body of the monster is filthy and impure. The Whore of Babylon is a siren calling to men, calling to the narrator John who stands amazed in the almost too near-distance. The Whore is reduced to a corpse and then ashes. No body parts remain, for these parts could lure us/John in for a closer look. The Whore is stripped of her layers of clothing. We look; we gaze (the male gaze); we do not turn away. Brooks states:

> The act of erotic transgression is a moment of heightened consciousness beyond the normal limits and conventions. The transgression of writing – another form of "communication" – is fundamentally similar; it assumes the impossible, as place and as state of being, a condition akin to mortal sin where pleasure is derived from the knowledge of *mal*, of one's wrongdoing, and knowledge itself is that pleasure.
>
> (1993: 277–8)

This body of the Whore is a semiotic sign to be possessed (Brooks 1993: 8). There is a different desire and eroticized body in the Apocalypse than in the Song of Songs. What is written on the body of the Whore? What text is violated, burned? The unveiling leads to the pleasures of horror.

Is the Apocalypse pornographic? Are apocalypses the pornography of the end of time? Pornography, like horror and utopian

Figure 6.3 The Whore of Babylon (1916) by Lovis Corinth, from his series of six lithographs on the Apocalypse of St John

literature, goes beyond societal boundaries. Like horror, pornography is iterative; the act of violence repeats itself in our re-readings, in the violence done on the psyche of the victim. Does the Apocalypse do psychological damage? The wrathful, judging God is alongside the joy (*jouissance*) of the believer. The deadly desire of godly utopia targets the unbeliever – and wayward women.

The Whore of Babylon smiles and shows pleasure in her torture and death scene in Lovis Corinth's vision. Holy whoredom was a spiritual way to union with the deity. The Whore considers herself a Queen Eve, Babel, the body of sacred prostitution. In a positive defense of prostitution, sex worker Cosi Fabian notes that "this absence of shame, this sense of the integrity of the Wondrous Vulva, is the most salient 'skill' that I bring to my work" (1997: 51). Fabian sees sacred prostitution, and her own work as a prostitute as sacred, as a space that exemplifies women's power. Although I do not agree with the ethics of her argument or profession, I think Fabian's point provides a different way of reading the Whore of Babylon. I am not claiming that Rome was not an evil imperial power; on the contrary, I think a political reading can be enhanced by dealing with the abused female symbolism in other ways than acceptance of the oppressive power as female. The voices of present-day prostitutes sound an interesting call to the past. Elisabeth Schüssler Fiorenza (1998: 93–4) tells me that I take the symbolism too literally. But what if a male prostitute was the symbol in the Apocalypse, and this male was raped and murdered? The symbolism matters, and the symbolism of a woman's body that is attacked is important. Would this symbol then be acceptable if the violence were imposed on a male? I think the gang rape and murder of a male would be totally unacceptable to biblical scholars and the "symbolism" of the evil empire would break down at this point.

In her linking of pornography and rape, Andrea Dworkin relates, "Prostitution is the all-encompassing condition, the body trapped in barter, the body imprisoned in commodity. They are crimes committed against women as women" (1983: 223). Dworkin's position is entirely different from that of Fabian, who wants to find a liberatory dimension to her chosen vocation. Is the Whore of Babylon yet another example of a woman who sleeps her way to the top? Is the alternative to be "saved through child-bearing" (1 Tim. 2: 15; Apoc. 12)? Are not the restrictions and gaze upon each pornographic in the sense of women being sexual objects of male desire?

How do modern definitions of pornography relate to a first-century text? The Minneapolis feminist antipornography ordinance defines pornography as the presentation of women as follows:

(a) as dehumanized as sexual objects, things, or commodities;
(b) as sexual objects who enjoy pain or humiliation;
(c) as sexual objects who experience sexual pleasure in being raped;
(d) as sexual objects tied up or cut up or mutilated or bruised or physically hurt;
(e) in postures of sexual submission or sexual servility, including inviting penetration;
(f) women's body parts – including but not limited to vaginas, breasts, and buttocks – are exhibited, such that women are reduced to those parts;
(g) as whores by nature;
(h) being penetrated by objects or animals;
(i) in scenarios of degradation, injury, torture, shown as filthy or inferior, bleeding, bruised, or hurt in a context that makes these conditions sexual.

(Barkey 1983: 1, see Richlin 1992: xv)

To use one example, is Lovis Corinth's lithograph of the Whore of Babylon pornographic? I would argue yes, but I think some forms of pornography are necessary to shock the reader/viewer into the realities of the degradation of women. Not all perversity is negative. Seeing the Apocalypse on the big screen, as it were, reveals the power of its images and puts the horror in one's face.

Other definitions of pornography are helpful in determining and evaluating the ethics of the Apocalypse. Amy Richlin's study of pornography in the classical world focuses on: "(1) inequity between partners; (2) objectification of women, with some emphasis on (a) nudity and (b) representation as food; (3) problematizing of the position of the female spectator" (1992: xviii). She examines the Greek word *pornographos*, "whore-writing." According to Nancy Rabinowitz, "The etymology of the word *pornography* – from *pornê* and *graphê*, depiction of whores – suggests that we should consider it in terms of both content and form." (1992: 37). She notes that like Catherine MacKinnon, Dworkin refuses to separate the representational from the material, rather seeing each as serving the other. Rabinowitz states:

In tragedy after tragedy, we see the female defined as sexual, possessed of a desire that destroys.... This brings me to another triangle, that among author, text, and audience. Here, I would argue, the audience is made masculine, asked to identify with the male protagonist, and in this way is put in relation to the author and the text. Through this experience masculine subjectivity is established. Tragedy participates in a pornographic structure of representation, accomplishing the solidification of the male subject at the expense of and through the construction of the female as object.

(1992: 51)

The Whore of Babylon becomes "the edible woman" (Margaret Atwood). The Whore is a femme fatale. In the Apocalypse the two major patriarchal institutions (earthly government and heavenly government) are represented as women. All female spaces are male controlled/dominated – Paradise and also the abyss. Both spaces are made perverse by the male gaze.

Jackson links pornography and horror: "Like pornography," gothic fiction "...functioned to supply an object of desire, to imagine social and sexual transgression" (Jackson 1981: 175). "The horror film, like pornography, dares not only to violate taboos but to expose the secrets of the flesh, to spill the contents of the body. If pornography is the genre of the wet dream, then horror is the genre of the wet death" (Pinedo 1997: 61). Pinedo points out that in pornography the wet dream is to be enacted, while the viewer remains distant from the death in the horror film. What of pornoapocalypse? What thrill (pleasure) is there in watching the violation of bodies, male and female, in the Last Judgment? Is the fantasy of revenge and ascetic/asthetic pain and suffering a draw for some Christians? Elaine Scarry describes, "To have pain is to have *certainty*; to hear about pain is to have *doubt*" (Scarry 1985: 13). Jesus is not the healing shaman of the gospels here; the nations are not healed but are scattered, as in some re-enactment scene of Babel – or Pentecost. The pain is bodily in the Apocalypse; believers will suffer death on earth but will participate in a heavenly wedding banquet (Apoc. 19) and live in eternal bliss in the heavenly city. "Death will be no more; mourning and crying and pain will be no more, for the first things have passed away" (Apoc. 21: 4). This pain is connected with sex. The desired utopia is gained through pain; both pornography and utopia go beyond societal boundaries. Perhaps the

Fantasy has been that the Bible has clear boundaries, an obvious ethic, an eventual just ending.

Anti-apocalypse

> ...the year 2000, in a certain way, will not take place.
>
> (Baudrillard 1989: 39)

A common critique of undergraduate students of the Apocalypse is that it is a weird narrative written by someone on hallucinogenic drugs. This narrative of the unknown – of chaos, demons, darkness, spirit beings, strange noises, and gruesome deaths – causes a reaction of masked revulsion. Why do my students want to avoid the Apocalypse? Why do the majority of biblical scholars avoid or marginalize this text? I think one key is in the horrific effect of apocalyptic literature. The theodicy of a deity gone mad, on a rampage of destruction, but all to create a pure nation of eternal bliss for the believers who follow God's plan, is overwhelming. The Apocalypse as horror is like a bomb threat; there may be no certainty that there is a real bomb, but the bomb "exists" enough to cause fears to surface and precautions to be taken.

The main ideological issue at stake with reading the Apocalypse through/as horror literature is over its social function. According to Schneider, "horror slashes through life's surfaces and exposes the heart of our condition. It cuts through all of our comforts, from the obvious to the sublime, and unveils our *rootlessness*. At the same time, it suggests a way to *handle* this rootlessness" (1993: 2). But in exposing our deepest fears does horror serve or subvert the status quo? Joseph Grixti says horror serves the status quo by bringing social fears to the surface. He quotes Sartre: "To experience any object as horrible, is to see it against the background of a world which reveals itself as *already* horrible" (Sartre 1962: 89, see Grixti 1989: 13). The world is horrible, so "myths are made (often sceptically, generally uncertainly) to perform the functions of magic" (1989: 184). Carroll thinks this social anxiety theory does not answer the question of horror's appeal. The horror genre is popular in times of crisis and in times of abundance, so that horror does not necessarily have to either subvert or affirm the status quo (1990: 248).

The majority thesis in studies of the Apocalypse is that it is a subversive narrative written in a time of political and religious crisis. God overthrows the colonial power, and the faithful are nonviolent participants (emphasis on participants) in the cosmic battle through their martyrdom. Is the Apocalypse a text of liberation and a text that subverts the dominant social order? In other words, is the Apocalypse a text that led/leads Christians to stand against the prevailing governmental evils? I think this reading is one of a multiplicity of ways of reading the Apocalypse. But horror theory suggests another reading that I think reveals the focus of fundamentalist and conservative Christian readings of the Apocalypse. Stephen King believes horror literature and film support the status quo: "horror fiction is really a Republican banker in a three-piece suit.... It has the effect of reconfirming values, of reconfirming self-image and our good feelings about ourselves" (quoted in Carroll 1990: 199). Carroll comments that "the confrontation and defeat of the monster in horror fictions might be systematically read as a restoration and defense of the established world view found in existing cultural schemas" (1990: 200). The evil monsters and all who follow their value system are eradicated.

In fundamentalist interpretations of the Apocalypse in the United States believers are told not to worry about or be responsible for the possible human ending of the world through nuclear accident or environmental pollution. The Rapture will occur first and all the believers will be taken up into the clouds with Jesus and will not suffer the tribulation on earth. Key to Jerry Falwell's apocalyptic vision is that the pusher of the nuclear button is God.[15] Right-wing, right hand of God – whose names are on the sacred scroll God holds? What is at stake is not the present working to avoid the Apocalypse, for it has already begun, and one must prepare and live for the future. The repetition of the story in the Apocalypse keeps the horror fresh. We have to make the end happen in fiction, because as Baudrillard says, *the very idea of the catastrophe is impossible* (1989: 37). There are some things we do not need to change in the social order to avoid the end, because God has everything under control already. On Trinity Broadcast Network one of the major themes of the 1990s is the persecution of Christians in the United States. The hint of the end time in the Apocalypse enables fundamentalist Christians to identify with the martyrs, but also with the vengeful heavenly hosts. Oh, the promise of watching the slaughter from the safety of heaven!

Lee Quinby uses the term "anti-apocalypse" to relate to the need for feminists to discard masculinist language and ways of thinking about the world. She concludes:

I am arguing, then, that feminism, even when oriented genealogically, will by definition always be implicated in apocalyptic desires for the end of (masculinist) time and the transcendence of (masculinist) space, including the space of the innately gendered body. Feminism can be, however, (and often is these days) *anti*-apocalyptic insofar as it is anti-essentialist, anti-universalist, and anti-eschatological.

(1994: 36)

The apocalyptic mind set is a masculine way of reading the social order and our (en)gendered place in that order. The prophecy of doom identifies with and participates in the apocalyptic violence. "Amen. Come, Lord Jesus!" (Apoc. 22: 20) marks the space of the future. This space is male space, a monstrous space of an abusing God. Where does the revolution against oppression lie? Why after the evil beasts are killed and the heavenly kingdom is established on earth is there still the sense of the horrible unknown? As horror, the Apocalypse leads us to hesitate at an ethical crossroads, certain of the evil of the dragon and his cohorts but uncertain of the goodness of God.

7

APOCALYPTIC FEAR

And in the beginning, then, was the word, the terror.
(Edward J. Ingebretsen 1996: x)

Introduction: cosmic fear

In a scene in the *Last Temptation of Christ* Jesus and John the Baptist are having a theological conversation in the desert. Jesus remarks, "You wanna know who my mother and father are? You wanna know who my God is? Fear. You look inside me and that's all you'll find." Fear of God, God as fear, fear of fear, fear of death, fear of the end of everything, fear as the driving force of faith – the Bible is full of fear. Popular interpretations of the Apocalypse of John capitalize on fear, drawing believers into the story of terror, only to emerge wanting to repeat the journey, desiring the final enactment of apocalypse.

Throughout the Bible are stories of fear and terror. Most of these stories center around fear of God and other supernatural beings (e.g. angels, the Son of Man, beasts). Traditional interpretations of the various words in Hebrew and Greek for fear promote the notion that fear is a part of respect and awe before the deity. Fear serves as a motivating factor for faith in both Judaism and Christianity. In this chapter I want to deconstruct the traditional readings of fear and read for the stories of fear where God is especially terrifying, in the apocalyptic stories. I want to explore the use of the words for fear in the Bible in their meanings of "terror" or "horror." I will be using horror theory, psychoanalytic theory, cultural criticism, and philosophical theories of the sublime to re-read for biblical terror.

Fear pervades the Bible. There is fear at the voice and majesty of God, and also at the presence of God (e.g. in the Garden of Eden). In other words, the character of God invokes terror in these texts. Fear is even deified in Genesis 31: 42 and 53: "So Jacob swore by

100

the Fear of his father Isaac ...." After John sees the Son of Man with a two-edged sword coming from his mouth his response is "I fell at his feet as though dead" (Apoc. 1: 17; cf. Dan. 8: 17). Deitiphobia is intense in some stories, especially when God enacts judgment or punishment. There are appearances of ghosts (Samuel summoned by the medium at Endor; the resurrected Jesus), and dead people rise (Lazarus). The reader can see the valley of dry bones (Ezek. 37), experience the devastation of Job, hear the screams of Jesus during his gruesome death on the cross (Mark 15: 37), and see the blood up to the horses' bridles (Apoc. 14: 20). This fantastic-marvelous and uncanny world in the Bible is full of angry and vengeful deities, angels, monsters, death, ghosts, and things that go bump at the end of the world. The horror is of great magnitude; there are no Gothic mansions here, but all of heaven and earth.

A spectre is haunting the Bible

H.P. Lovecraft's famous quote is instructive in defining fear: "The oldest and strongest emotion of mankind is fear, and the oldest and strongest kind of fear is fear of the unknown" (1973: 12). In the New Testament the Greek forms of *phobia* occur 158 times. Fear is a major theme when imagining or being face-to-face with the divine. The root meanings of the Greek include: "to flee," "being startled," "running away," "apprehension," "sudden and violent fear," "fright," "panic" (Kittel and Friedrich 1964–74: 189–90). "The subject of fear in the [Hebrew Bible] is almost always man" (1964–74: 200). "Hence evaluation of the reaction of fear is closely bound up with the understanding of one's own existence. It also offers access to the religious self-understanding of specific individuals and groups" (1964–74: 192). In Greek mythology there is the god Phobos, a powerful war-god (1964–74: 191–2).

One prominent Bible dictionary defines "fear of the Lord" as "the awe that a person ought to have before God (Prov 5: 7; Eccles. 12: 13). As such it can be said to constitute 'true religion' (Ps 34: 11).... However, it may also carry overtones of judgment (2 Cor 5: 11; 1 Pet 1: 17)" (Achtemeier 1985: 305).

Todorov states that "The uncanny realizes... only one of the conditions of the fantastic: the description of certain reactions, especially of fear" (1973: 47). As horror categories, in the uncanny events are seen as rational, whereas in the fantastic-uncanny supernatural events are explained in the end (1973: 44). Apocalyptic literature does not give a rational explanation for the horrors it

Figure 7.1 The appropriate response of fear: *John Falling as though Dead before the Son of Man* by Silvan Otmar (Augsburg, 1523)

inflicts upon the reader. Eric Rabkin relates: "Horror fiction... in its creation of supernatural or otherworldly terrors, contradicts possibility quite often. In this sense in which horror fiction is more radically fantastic than pornography, it is both more radically escapist and more radically revealing" (1976: 50). Apocalyptic horror connects with the most fearful emotions and heightens the sense that the end is near. Both Daniel and John instruct the reader how to respond: "As for me, Daniel, my spirit was troubled within me, and the visions of my head terrified me" (Dan. 7: 15) and "my thoughts greatly terrified me, and my face turned pale; but I kept the matter in my mind" (Dan. 7: 28); "When I saw him [the Son of Man], I fell at his feet as though dead" (Apoc. 1: 17).

All the supernatural beings in the Apocalypse are terrifying. The Son of Man with the strange body parts is the central figure of the kingdom of heaven. He appears as sword-wielding Son of Man, as Messianic child, and as a Lamb – morphing his way through the story. This Christ becomes for later Docetists a Dracula-like figure, a phantom, a ghost, or as Moretti describes Dracula: "a saver, an ascetic, an upholder of the Protestant ethic. And in fact he has no body, or rather, he has no shadow" (1988: 91). Christ haunts the Apocalypse in many forms, and one of these forms is as a powerful, ghostly figure, resurrecting from the dead in different bodily forms. For Rudolf Otto one aspect of the "holy" or numinous is the awe, fear, and dread of ghosts. Otto defines this feeling at a ghostly encounter "as that of 'grue', grisly horror" (1978: 28). "*Ghost*, in Middle English *goste*, meant 'frightening' before it came to mean the thing that frightens" (Barzun 1986: xix). Ghost stories are popular because they are about a curious Other that "belongs to an absolutely different [reality], and which at the same time arouses an irrepressible interest in the mind" (1986: 29). Otto traces the history of religious dread or awe:

> Its antecedent stage is "daemonic dread" (cf. the horror of Pan) with its queer perversion, a sort of abortive offshoot, the "dread of ghosts." It first begins to stir in the feeling of "something uncanny," "eerie," or "weird." It is this feeling which, emerging in the mind of primeval man, forms the starting-point for the entire religious development in history. "Daemons" and "gods" alike spring from this root, and all the products of "mythological apperception" or "fantasy" are nothing but different modes in which it has been objectified.
>
> (1978: 14–15)

Otto is saying that in the experience of the "mysterium tremendum," human fear takes on a different mode and is not like "natural terror." The distinction between natural and uncanny fear is clear for Otto: "I may be beyond all measure afraid and terrified without there being even a trace of the feeling of uncanniness in my emotion" (1978: 16). The Wholly Other of either demons or gods evokes a range of emotions from pleasure to terror. The possibility of God's wrath (Gk. *orgé*) governs human emotions. Otto relates: "...that the idea of the wrath of God in the Bible is always a synthesis.... Something supra-rational throbs and gleams, palpable and visible, in the 'wrath of God,' prompting to a sense of 'terror' that no 'natural' anger can arouse" (1978: 19). In other words, the supernatural evokes irrational feelings. The presence of God brings a different kind of awe – one mixed with dread and terror at the possibility of God's wrath.

Apocalypse is about fear and desire. James Hillman discusses the difference between the god of war, Mars, and the Christian God:

> Apocalypse is inherent, not in the Martial deity, but in the Christian deity. Fascination with a transcendent Christ may be more the threat to the Christian civilization than the War God himself. Are not civilizations saved by their Gods also led to destruction by those same, their own, Gods?
>
> (1987: 129)

The holy war of the Apocalypse is the imagination of ultimate violence. The time of the god Mars is in the spring, a time of beginnings. Even through the destruction of human war there exists the possibility of renewal. But the idea of apocalypse provides the end of possibilities: "The Apocalypse may lift veils, but it closes down into the truly final solution, after which there is no reopening, no *recorso*. Broken the wheel" (Hillman 1987: 130). The biblical Apocalypse is open, repeatable, forever pointing to the possibility of ultimate brokenness, closure.

The Apocalypse is full of eternal monsters. The monsters of capitalism, Frankenstein and Dracula (Moretti 1988: 89), are different from the monsters of the Apocalypse. Moretti points out that these two monsters are *"totalizing* monsters" (1988: 84) who never appear together:

> The threat would be too great: and this literature, having produced terror, must also erase it and restore peace. It

must restore the broken equilibrium, giving the illusion of
being able to stop history: because the monster expresses
the anxiety that the future will be monstrous.

(1988: 83–4)

(Since Moretti's book the two monsters have appeared together in
movies produced for television.)

In a Marxist view the Frankenstein and Dracula monsters represent the owners and the workers in the class struggle. Moretti adds:
"The literature of terror is born precisely *out of the terror of a split
society*, and out of the desire to heal it" (1988: 83). But as Mary
Shelley shows that *"capitalism has no future"* in the Frankenstein
monster (Moretti 1988: 89), so too does the Apocalypse show us
that the monstrous (pre-capitalist) imperial power of earth will have
no future. The kings and merchants, and the beasts that support
them, will all be overthrown and violently defeated. This defeat is
in the form of mutilation; the birds of midheaven gorge themselves
on the flesh of the mighty (Apoc. 19: 17–21), and the beast and the
false prophet are thrown into "the lake of fire that burns with
sulfur" (19: 20) where "they will be tormented day and night
forever and ever" (20: 10). This notion of eternal torment increases
the horror.

The Apocalypse throws all the monsters into its story of the
terror of the end of time. No one can escape God's judgment. The
monsters bump against each other, the other characters, and the
reader; it is a crowded narrative. Everywhere the reader turns there
is a supernatural being enacting supernatural acts, the (bad?) breath
of the monsters down your back. It is enough to make the skin
crawl, one's blood turn cold, one's skin turn pale, and one's hair to
stand on end. The Apocalypse lacks subtlety; all-out gore grabs the
reader's attention – and emotions. Even more, apocalyptic horror
produces the bone-deep experience of fear. As Otto describes the
"shudder" that occurs with a deep experience of the uncanny, "The
'shudder' reappears in a form ennobled beyond measure where the
soul, held speechless, trembles inwardly to the farthest fibre of its
being" (1978: 16). This shudder of fear is the response of both dread
and desire.

In the Apocalypse both the evil and the faithful experience torture
and death. Anyone who does not have "the seal of God on their foreheads" (Apoc. 9: 4) is tortured for five months by locust beasts with
scorpion stings (9: 5). The torment is extreme: "And in those days
people will seek death but will not find it; they will long to die, but

death will flee from them" (9: 6). The messianic Lamb was slaughtered. Martyrdom is an option for the faithful, bringing eternal reward in the end, but these witnesses (Gk. *marturo*) suffer death (2: 13; 11). As a "viewer" of these horrors, I want to shout simultaneously "Don't break the seal!" (out of fear of the gore) and "Break the seal!" (out of curiosity) to the narrator/character John. In the lectionary canon of my own religious background, the Episcopal Church, the seals are never broken, scrolls never opened, trumpets never sounded, the vials never poured. Only heavenly hymns are sung, with the door to heaven opened wide enough to peak in on the grandeur.

Freud thought that fear came from a person repressing emotions. Moretti explains "that the perturbing element is *within them*: that it is they themselves that produce the monsters they fear" (1988: 102). One looks in the mirror and sees one's own face as the face of the monster. For Moretti one should not fear going mad: "No, one should be afraid of the *monster*, of something *material*, something *external*" (1988: 102). Fear works in the repressed reaches of the human mind. The Apocalypse plays on that repressed fear about the wrath of God, the presence of evil in the world (false prophets, evil kings), and the end of the world. The unthinkable becomes thinkable. At the level of the thinkable a decision must be made: to be children (in the image) of God or children (in the image) of the beasts (the female figures of Jezebel and the Whore are included here). Evil appears very seductively (Jezebel and especially the Whore), and one has to choose wisely and carefully. As in Moretti's study of Gothic monsters, the monsters in the Apocalypse are "terrorizing metaphors" (1988: 105) that have multiple meanings but lead to a dialectical choice.

The end of the world is irrational. The numinous bounds in, taking over every space. The means to the end in the Apocalypse narrative is fear. According to Moretti, "For fear to arise, reason must be made insecure... [readers] are dragged forcibly *into* the text; the characters' fear is also theirs" (1988: 107).

> To think for oneself, to follow one's own interests: these are the real dangers that this literature wants to exorcise. Illiberal in a deep sense, it mirrors and promotes the desire for an integrated society, a capitalism that manages to be "organic".... It is a fear one *needs*: *the* price one pays for coming contentedly to terms with a social body based on irrationality and menace. Who says it is escapist?
>
> (1988: 108)

Of course, the Apocalypse differs from the Dracula and Frankenstein stories in that the monsters of good and evil do battle and "good" wins out over "evil" in the end. An integrated society is created; not a capitalist society, but a paradise in the form of the New Jerusalem. The Apocalypse is a literature of terror in the extreme, but then its topic (the end of the world) is extreme.

Nietzsche thought of the Apocalypse as "The most rabid outburst of vindictiveness in all recorded history" (1956: 185, quoted in Hays 1996: 169). In his study of New Testament ethics Richard Hays comments:

> Those who follow him in persecution and death are not filling a randomly determined quota of martyrs; rather, they are enacting the will of God, who has chosen to overcome evil precisely in and through righteous suffering, not in spite of it. That is why those who bear the name of the Lamb on their foreheads must also share his fate.
>
> (1996: 179)

"Finally, the ethical staying power of the Apocalypse is a product of its *imaginative richness*" (1996: 184). This "imaginative richness" may well be the "staying power" that Hays notes. But this power is over the top, a deity gone wild, not on the side of love but of hate and vindictiveness, inducing earthly terror to gird the glory of heaven. The real terror is that the torture never ceases; the tortures of the abyss are endless. From the Apocalypse through the next 2,000 years of Christianity the terrors of hell increase. That is where the real "imaginative richness" can be found; in subsequent apocalypses and journeys of hell, God becomes more and more dangerous. Hays's defense of the ethics of the Apocalypse seems to me like the defense that someone in "the family" would give; it has a Mafiaesque feel to it.

Who's afraid of the big, bad God?

> The only natural predator is God.
> (TV ad for the October 1997 *House of Frankenstein 1997*)

Imagine that God is a mad scientist who created all creatures, both good and evil. God owns the factory and can mass produce all creatures, including monsters. God is an exotic monster, a space alien, head of an alien nation (heaven). Since some of the creatures (natural and supernatural) are bound to turn against God, a holy war must continually be fought until the final battle at the end of time. Mostly, it is a cold war, since the Devil dwells in his own, separate, opposite kingdom (hell). But this war is costly and time consuming. Good and evil are clearly defined and represented. But both beings are incredibly violent.

Denise Levertov echoes the violence in her poem, *Age of Terror*: "Between the fear / of the horror of Afterwards / and the despair / in the thought of no Afterwards / we move abraded, / each gesture scraping us / on the millstones" (1987: 64). For Stephen King:

> Terror – what Hunter Thompson calls "fear and loathing" – often arises from a pervasive sense of disestablishment; that things are in the unmaking. If that sense of unmaking is sudden and seems personal – if its hits you around the heart – then it lodges in the memory as a complete set.
>
> (1983: 9)

Dramatic presentations of the Apocalypse around Hallowe'en by conservative, evangelical Christian churches are meant to imprint this terror. Mock abortions and the terror of hell are shown with as much gore as possible. These "Tribulation Trails" are a chance to get close to the horror, to put one's hands in the (fake) blood.

I recently went on a field trip to a "Tribulation Trail" with my "Apocalypse and Revolution" class. We chose the biggest one in the Atlanta area, at a suburban church that guides about 18,000 visitors through their version of the Tribulation. In grand pre-millennialist style, the background for the trail is that God comes and "takes out the Church" (the Rapture), and those left behind experience the rule of the Anti-Christ until Christ returns for the final judgment. Sites on the trail include a speech by Death; a video of world scenes accompanied by contemporary Christian music about going "home" (the video ends with scenes from a Promise Keepers rally); the Four Horsemen (on real horses) shouting warnings to us; scenes of crime and degradation; graves unearthed from which the believers were raptured; cannibalism; a concentration camp in which Christians were executed; an opportunity to receive "the mark of the Beast" (a glow-in-the-dark 666 on the top of our hands); and scenes of pain, suffering, and great need. Jesus appears only twice, and he is removed from earth and is standing on a platform; once he judges the Anti-Christ (world military leader), and then he judges people as he stands next to a great throne. On our visit we witnessed the judgment of a couple who had been married for forty-five years. The husband was immediately taken to heaven. The wife had to argue her case before Jesus; she had been in the church all her life and had done good things as a member of the Sierra Club (!). Her pleas were ineffectual; Jesus condemned her to hell, and the angels took her away. The whole effect of the trail is to produce fear; horses rushing at you, demons sliming on you, loud guns going off next to you, judgments being pronounced on you. In wonderful post-modern style, the terrors are re-enacted multiple times as groups proceed at about 20-minute intervals. For example, as we stood at the grave site, the Four Horsemen made their charge once again. There is an emphasis on the repeatability of the stories, over and over, until, of course, it gets to be late and the church members/actors go home.

"Realize, Repent, Receive" we are told at the last station of the trail; a decision at the end to follow Jesus would be timely. As Ingebretsen notes, "Fear, then, keeps a community vigilant, and in that word we should hear yet one more theological echo: vigil" (1996: xxiv). The emphasis is other worldly, not this worldly, and all it takes to gain salvation is accepting Jesus into your heart. If you reject Jesus, you are doomed to experience the terrors of the (near) future. Accept Jesus, and you will be on the side of the God who enacts all the terrors; you can view the torture and destruction from the safety and comfort of heaven. But not everyone knows how to read the signs of the times; where would the apocalyptic fun be if all were saved? Ingebretsen relates, "In either the semiotics of grace *or* the grotesque, not everyone is saved; not everyone can read rightly the signs" (1996: 198). The Rapture only works if there is the Tribulation; the benefits of heaven are never seen, only the terror to be inflicted on those who are not in God's "camp."

This rather campy experience of the literary tradition shows the link between desire and dread. Clive Barker remarks that "There is no delight the equal of dread" (quoted in Hartwell 1992: 1). As cynical participants in the Tribulation Trail, my class could laugh at many of the attempts to instill fear, thus creating distance between us and the story being acted out before us.

In apocalyptic literature the transcendent that the believer desires becomes personal, so the reader must make a personal decision about which monsters to support. I discovered an excellent example of this desire to be near the God that both cares and enacts wrath in an antique store in East Atlanta: a wooden plaque with the message, "Lord God (S)cares." The original carving was "God Cares," but someone added the extra connecting letters. Lord God (S)cares is the resulting message. Preachers during the Protestant Reformation and the later Puritan period emphasized the need for fear, especially fear of death.[1]

In her study of Gothic horror, Judith Halberstam describes the merging of desire and fear in Gothic novels: "Characters in these novels both fear and desire the monster's monstrosity; on a very general level, they desire it because it releases them from the constraints of an ordered life and they fear it because it reveals the flimsy nature of human identity" (1995: 112). Halberstam also notes the "gendered grammar of fear" that gives rise to both misogyny and homophobia. In the Apocalypse one of the false prophets, Jezebel, and one of the main monsters, the Whore of Babylon, are both female. The text accuses both of sexual perversion. Deviant behavior (like the evils acted out on the Tribulation Trail) is necessary for God's plan to be fulfilled. Halberstam advises, "If, however, we are able to separate monstrosity from sexual perversion, this may lead to the possibility of an antihomophobic and anti-essentialist theory of the representation of fear and violence"

Figure 7.2 Lord God Scares: southern folk art on a wooden plaque

(1995: 112). But in the Apocalypse, monstrosity and sexual perversion are linked. Fear takes on an erotic edge; the monsters are to be feared and desired all at once.

Such fear is centered on the body and on violence on the body. In the Apocalypse there is what in horror films is called the "gross out" in terms of bodily (and earthly) horror. Consider two scenes, the murder of the Whore and the deaths of the mighty:

> And the ten horns that you saw, they and the beast will hate the whore; they will make her desolate and naked; they will devour her flesh and burn her up with fire.
>
> (Apoc. 17: 16)

> Then I saw an angel standing in the sun, and with a loud voice he called to all the birds that fly in midheaven, "Come, gather for the great supper of God, to eat the flesh of kings, the flesh of captains, the flesh of the mighty, the flesh of horses and their riders – flesh of all, both free and slave both small and great." ... These two [the beast and false prophet] were thrown alive into the lake of fire that burns with sulfur. And the rest were killed by the sword of the rider on the horse, the sword that came from his mouth; and all the birds were gorged with their flesh.
>
> (Apoc. 19: 17–18, 20–21)

Over the death of the Whore there is much crying by the mighty ones who observe the horror from a distance "in fear of her torment" (18: 10 and 15). An angel turns the rivers to blood: "Because they shed the blood of saints and prophets, you have given them blood to drink. It is what they deserve!" (18: 6), and fire, plagues, earthquakes, hail, and darkness are added to the terror. The mouth of the dragon emits frog-like spirits to assemble the world at Armageddon (18: 13–16). The judgment scene is intense. As Pinedo recognizes in horror films, "Violence is random, yet specifically aimed against the body to produce an 'intimate apocalypse'" (1997: 65). All the gory details of torture and suffering are given. As the bowls poured forth, "people gnawed their tongues in agony, and cursed the God of heaven because of their pains and sores, and they did not repent of their deeds" (18: 10–11). The cry echoes throughout the Apocalypse, "For the great day of their wrath has come, and who is able to stand?" (6: 17). No *body* can stand is the answer. The Apocalypse is full of bodies – martyrs under the altar; two witnesses

111

dead and then resurrected in the city street; bodies of angels, beasts, and other supernatural beings; believers and unbelievers. Some are victims and some are survivors; the body count is high. Pinedo is instructive here, "In horror, the involuntary spasm is the death of the penetrated or devoured body accompanied by screaming and bleeding, the visual proof of violation. Unlike porn, in horror it is the penetrated body of the victim that shudders and bleeds..." (1997: 62). The Apocalypse is both intimate and global; the violence is both like the slasher film (e.g. Freddie Krueger in the *Nightmare on Elm Street* films) where individual bodies are targeted, and the apocalypse of the earth where no one survives (e.g. *Dr Strangelove*; the dream scene of nuclear apocalypse in *Terminator 2: Judgement Day*). The earthly beasts in the Apocalypse inflict great pain, but it is God who destroys the whole earth.

Pinedo makes the point that "horror produces a bounded experience of fear" in which the repressed fears of everyday life are exposed and enacted (1997: 17; 38–9). She describes "recreational terror" as creating a fiction of horror in which the collapse of the social order is contained in the body. Pinedo refers to this phenomenon as "the spectacle of the ruined body" (1997: 6). According to Pinedo, "The experience of terror is bounded by the tension between proximity and distance, reality and illusion" (1997: 40). The narrative of the biblical Apocalypse, like a horror film, provides a "contained experience" (Pinedo 1997: 41) in order for the viewer to have mastery over the experience, but like many horror films, there is no neat closure; the terror is always out there, ready to strike at any moment.[2] Prophecy reporters on Trinity Broadcast Network revel in this proximity of the end time. There is a sense of real joy in their voices as they announce the world events that "support" the Bible's symbolism. These prophets of doom want to invade the order with their tales of terror. They shudder with glee as they tell these fearful stories. The promise of the Apocalypse is that the shudder is eternal; the "little death" becomes the big death; the terror never ends; the monsters still roam loose (on earth and in heaven).

Conclusion: the necessity of fear

It happens when the story dies. The evil is set free.
(Wes Craven in *Wes Craven's New Nightmare*)

The stories that generate apocalyptic fear have to be told and retold to ward off the evil. Placing the Apocalypse at the end of the biblical canon acts as a sort of amulet, a magical token keeping God's judgment at a distance – as long as the story continues to be told. The end of the Apocalypse opens into another apocalypse and on and on. The big crunch prophesied by physicists to occur billions of years from now is too distant and hard to grasp; it is necessary to imagine a more immediate, intimate, end of everything. The terror needs to be more concrete, more specific, more extreme. There is a need to watch the torture in the Apocalypse, hear the cries, see the blood, feel the fire. In the excesses of the Apocalypse the reader can look in vain for the excesses of a deity of love and compassion. And despite the claims of the text, there is no excess of justice here, only the excess of violence and the fear of violence.

What does the excess of fear in the Apocalypse tell us about the Christian religion? Or, as Pinedo asks of the horror film, "How does it help us to develop strategies for bringing about progressive social change?" (1997: 3). This question is about the ethics of reading the ethics of the text, and I want to question the ethics of the text as I question the ethics of my own reading. Traditional ways of reading the Apocalypse for ethical strategies (such as the one from Hays) disturb me; I feel the text has too much control over me and the current, more intimate apocalypses in my own culture become more distant. I want to loosen the hold of the Apocalypse, to negotiate its rough terrains. Another way to put this is that I want a critical dialogue not a monologue of "Truth" and what the text "means" or "intends." The exegetical ends are not neat; the interpretation is as messy as the text.

How do readers manage/control the Apocalypse? Here are a few ways:

1   Render the Apocalypse at the bottom of the New Testament "hierarchy" (Gospels, Acts, Pauline and non-Pauline epistles – delineating high-brow and low-brow texts) and ignore it. (The Apocalypse is verifiably low-brow if it is compared to horror literature and film!)
2   Diagnose the author as mentally disturbed.
3   Study the text as a cultural artifact, as cultural camp (through horror films and other contemporary art forms).
4   Seek to control it by pin-pointing the historical context of the text (if the text is linked effectively to the past, it is neutralized).

5   Enact the drama of the text as an evangelizing tool (e.g. Tribulation Trail).
6   Use the text as a political manifesto for revolutionary situations (e.g. Ernesto Cardinal's poem, *The Apocalypse*, about the civil war in Nicaragua).

There are many ways to attempt to rein in the reign of apocalyptic terror. But this exclusivistic and violent tale is part of "sacred scripture," not merely a mode of cultural escapism or a mode of expressing a culture's repressed fears and desires. The end of the Bible is connected with its beginning; Ingebretsen believes that "the Apocalypse does not come at the *end* of time, as is conventionally thought. Its terror lies behind, not ahead" (1996: ix). I agree that the terror is not relegated to the end of the biblical story; fear of the power and wrath of God is there from the beginning. However, in disagreement with Ingebretsen I would say that apocalyptic fear breaks the boundaries of a linear space–time continuum; the terror lies behind, ahead, violating all the set canonical boundaries – engaging in multiple terrors, multiple fears, created and re-created at every turn, with every reading and performance. In an intuitive mode, the text jumps out at me like Freddie Krueger from the closet in *New Nightmare*: "Miss me?" Apocalypse is not a neat, contained genre. The thread of the apocalyptic is in all the narratives of nationalism, war, exile, judgment, and gospel, woven throughout both testaments. Of course, there is hope for the future – that the earthly monsters/enemies will be defeated – but the price is (once again, as in the flood) the destruction of the earth by a wrathful God.

Maurice Blanchot talks of fear – fear of death, fear of fear, fear of nothingness, nothing to fear. Fear is ancient and has always been with humans:

> *You would have said in vain: I do not believe in fear; this too ancient fear, without idolatry, without figure and without faith, the beyond of fear that does not affirm itself in any beyond, would again push you into the narrow streets, eternal,* without end, towards *the daily meeting, that which does not propose itself to you as an end; whence the fact that, even making your way there every day, you are never there. "Because I reach it by flight, fleeing it endlessly."*
>
> *"You respect fear. – Perhaps, but it does not respect me, it has no regard."* The most serious of idolatries: to have regard for that which has no regard.
>
> (1992: 134)

Fear, awe, and dread at the final hour; fear is all that is left. Fear, the Fear, is responsible for both the creation and destruction of the world. The Fear came to earth and was crucified and resurrected. What lurks in the nooks and crannies of the text, and of the theologies and hermeneutics of the Apocalypse? What is there exactly to be afraid of? The magic still exists in the Apocalypse; how God is going to enact the disaster remains a mystery. According to the text, the proper response to this unknown future is fear.

Are readers then condemned to be eternal victims of the Apocalypse? Judith Halberstam is instructive in her warnings of viewing horror films (in particular, *A Nightmare on Elm Street*), "It is when you cease to watch yourself watching that you become the victim" (1995: 146). She gives two main "techniques of spectatorship": "First, horror depends upon energy directed at the screen, not just energy directed at the viewer – you are only scared if you want to be. Second, readings of monsters *can* disable them" (1995: 146). When asked to describe his worst fear, Wes Craven relates, "With a horror film it allows you [to] attach a visual identification to an unnamed fear or series of fears, and gives you a story in which it's confronted and defeated" (Simulchat 1997: 7). One of my reactions to Tribulation Trail was, "Keep telling the story, to keep the terror away!" Perhaps the Apocalypse has this value: an emotional release (catharsis) of our deepest fears. But such a rationalization of the power of this text is naive, ignoring the violence the Apocalypse glorifies, and the glorious roles God, Jesus, the angels, and the saints have making "the end" a reality. New readings are called for – new retellings of the story to disable the monsters of death and destruction.

As another alternative reading of the Apocalypse, consider the following "pictures" of the terror, from the 13 November 1995 *Newsweek*; the article is entitled, "Do We Need Satan?" (One of the students in my "Apocalypse and Revolution" class this semester, Jennifer Long, included these pictures in her journal.) First is Nazi Germany, a picture of Hitler at a public event in 1934 juxtaposed with a fourteenth-century representation of sinners at the Last Judgment. Second, two details are side by side: Hans Memling's *The Last Judgment* next to the memorial to the Pol Pot victims in Cambodia at the Choenung extermination camp. Third is the pit of hell (Dirck Bouts's fifteenth-century painting) and a mass grave in the genocide of Rwanda (in which an estimated 1 million people were massacred in a three-month period in spring 1994; this particular pit is of Hutu refugees, although the majority of the murdered were Tutsi). *Newsweek*'s understanding of evil and fear in this article is to place contemporary horrors next to the horrors of hell. Are fictional monsters necessary in our culture to help us manage the extent of human evil? Do we need a character of God who is capable of the most horrible deeds imaginable (the flood, the fire, Apocalypse), in order to defeat these "lesser monsters," real and imagined? For the organizers of Tribulation Trail, these contemporary genocides are an integral (and necessary) part of God's plan for the end. But for those connected to the suffering (through a personal connection or through conscientization), these events are embodied terror, embodied apocalypse. "Who is able to stand" in the face of such terror?

Native American poet Joy Harjo relates the genocide of her ancestors to fear. She proclaims, "I release you, fear, because you hold / these scenes in front of me and I was born / with eyes that can never close." Should the Apocalypse give us "eyes that can never close?" Should the Apocalypse be a memory, a reality, but not an inevitable future? Can there be a critical reading that stands face-to-face with the horror, offering a counter-revolution to the biblical one? "Who is able to stand?" And who can face the fear? Again, Harjo offers instruction on facing fear; facing fear involves the body:

> Oh, you have choked me, but I gave you
> the leash.
> You have gutted me but I gave you the knife.
> You have devoured me, but I laid myself
> across the fire.
>
> I take myself back, fear.
> You are not my shadow any longer.
> I won't hold you in my hands.
> You can't live in my eye, my ears, my voice
> my belly, or in my heart my heart
> my heart my heart
> But come here, fear
> I am alive and you are so afraid
> of dying.
>
> (from Joy Harjo 1983, "I Give You Back")

8

CONCLUSION: THE JOY OF (APOCALYPTIC) SEX

Just because it's a love story doesn't mean you can't have a decapitation or two.

(the actor who plays Freddie in *Wes Craven's New Nightmare*, 1994)

The biblical God is the supreme embodiment of hegemonic hypermasculinity, and as such the object of universal adoration.

(Moore 1996: 139)

The sacred surrounds and enslaves us.... The Church is sacred.

(Genet 1963: 344)

The Apocalypse's canonical status does give it a special religious and cultural power. But why is violence condoned when it is in scripture and when God is the actor? This book troubles me in different ways than it troubled the Eastern churches in the fourth century CE or Martin Luther in the Protestant Reformation. The problems of holy war, ecocide, gynocide, and the portrayal of the deities as wrathful powers just will not go away. I see the Apocalypse as a misogynist male fantasy of the end of time (1992: 105). On this note, a feminist biblical scholar at a conference several years ago proposed that I work through my "no" to the text to get to "yes." My response was and is that I want to say "no" to this text, for ultimately, I do not find the Apocalypse to be a liberating story.

I want to address three major issues that come out of the responses to my work over the last five years. First of all, a postmodern reading enables a reader to enter the text at multiple points or gaps. I imagine the Apocalypse as a type of hypertext, and I can

117

enter the imaginary (fantastic) world of the text/story wherever I can imagine an opening. For example, I could choose to enter at any of the following points:

gender	war	ecocide
violence	New Jerusalem	throne
beasts	Babylon	gynocide
Jezebel	angels	abyss
trance	fear	fire
hymns	robes	Pergamum
eating	mouth	vomit

Of course, there are many other openings into this text, and some are openings of openings (abyss, mouth). Apocalypse is the ultimate never-ended story; chaos is re-created and scattered over the universe. These apocalyptic scatterings are what I am learning to read in my culture. The multiple texts and images of apocalypse that are present speak in different languages, the tongues of doom, the voices of heaven. With every new entry into the biblical text, I must learn new languages – autobiographical and ideological criticisms, fantasy and horror theories, the discourses of race, class, and sexualities.

In this postmodern interdisciplinary place in which I find myself, I am often overwhelmed by the possibilities. In my work on the Apocalypse I have chosen to drop some baggage, precisely the baggage I lug into my college classes (the historical-critical method, socio-political context, date, authorship, etc.) and take on other baggage (semiotics, Marxist feminist critical theories, deconstruction, fantasy theories, etc.). I am resisting the master (pun intended) narrative and the traditional reading strategies, not in order to set up yet another master narrative but to create another site/space for a resisting reading. The apocalyptic text is a map, a landscape with many ruptures and tears (especially the abyss), and there is still so much unexplored territory. The kind of postmodern reading that begins, for example, in the abyss, is not nihilistic, for there are possibilities and different visions which are unattainable by historically grounded biblical exegesis.

Second, I want to play with this disturbing text because it has religious and cultural holds on Christianity and on Western culture. And this postmodern reading is not apolitical or unconcerned with the ethical (a common critique of postmodernism), but rather embedded in the reality of the heteroglossic readings and misreadings (e.g. David Koresh) of the Apocalypse. My reading is always in process, never completed and never arrived.

My third concern is the largest. On the issue of sexual/erotic desire in the Apocalypse, I am drawing from a large body of work on desire and eroticism in texts. There are many bodies in the Apocalypse, male and female (and some ambiguous in terms of gender and sexuality), and these bodies act and are acted upon in various ways. Women's bodies are particularly abused in this text; women's bodies are also desired.[1] Peter Brooks explains, "those stories we tell about the body in the effort to know and to have it, which result in making the body a site of significa- tion – the place for the inscription of stories – and itself a signifier, [are] a prime agent in narrative plots and meaning" (1993: 5–6). By desire I do not mean simply a focus on genitalia or the sexual act but the unconscious desire for erotic power. One criticism of my work has been to point out that John is more interested in the city than the body when describing the Bride as the New Jerusalem, but I am more interested in what happens to the body of the female in the text – the Bride is made into polis, city, the Whore gang raped and burned and eaten, the Woman Clothed with the Sun is a reproductive vessel who is exiled subsequent to giving birth, and Jezebel is destroyed. What is positive about this vision? I would imagine a positive role for women in the Apocalypse would instead be storming the patriarchal heaven.

Another possible reading for desire is that the final vision is homoerotic. The 144,000 men become the Bride of Christ and/or the Bride becomes the 144,000 men. J. Michael Clark, one of the co-founders of the American Academy of Religion's Gay Men's Theology Group, wrote to me in a letter concerning homoeroticism in the Apocalypse:

> I found myself doing a gay man's reading of your text. I kept wondering what, if anything, this particularly vexing biblical book has to say to gay men (and lesbians as *gay*; since you have them covered as sexual women). I was espe- cially struck by the latent homoeroticism of the 144,000, insofar as the apocalyptic utopia seems to depend on male bonding and male-only space. At the same time, all the discourse of desire is, as you point out, very heterosexist – men desiring women whom they are not supposed to have (to have the Bride would make her a Whore). The impetus

Figure 8.1 The erotic horrors of hell by Dieric Bouts (1410–75), *Descent into Hell*

is clearly toward a celibate world of saved, but sexless, none the less heterosexual men – a movement toward the death of (sexual) desire! A dreary utopia, indeed!

(private correspondence, October 1993)

Nothing is stable in the Apocalypse, especially gender and desire. The evil will continue to do evil, and the abyss of creation/chaos remains a tear in the text, (Derrida's postcard or ruptured hymen). Perhaps I do not have the same religious investment in the Apocalypse as have others in traditional biblical studies. Fredric Jameson remarked to me that the Apocalypse is so blatantly sexist and violent that it is an easy target.[2] I do not want to substitute a female heavenly warrior for a male one. Both the good and evil forces in this book are horrifying beasts that invoke cosmic fear. The Apocalypse is full of terror and torture. I resist this ancient text, as I resist contemporary contexts of horror.

Sexuality in the Apocalypse is complex. First, there is the male gaze on the sexually active female, either Jezebel and the Whore or the Virgin who gives birth (Apoc. 12) and the Bride of Christ. Then there are the 144,000 virginal men who enter into the Bride of Christ/New Jerusalem; I referred to this scene as "mass intercourse" in my earlier book (1992: 80). The husband, Christ/Lamb of God, allows (wills?) this entering, after which the 144,000 men become the Bride. The Bride becomes the holy city Jerusalem (Apoc. 21: 9 ff.). I now think that the 144,000 do not want to have the Bride but instead want to *be* the Bride. These faithful servants of God "reign forever and ever" (Apoc. 22: 5), so they must have thrones also. Are the 144,000 "Queens" of heaven? Is their desire to be Brides of Christ? Or to usurp the Whore's queenly power and position? Keller relates, "we may behold the Whore of Babylon as a great 'queen' indeed: imperial patriarchy in drag" (1996: 77). So is the Whore actually the male city-state in drag? What "vested interests" are there in such cross-dressing (in "fine linen, bright and pure" in 19: 8 and all the precious jewels and plants of heaven in Chapters 21–2)? What is really happening in the "Rapture"?

M.H. Abrams brings out the concept of Christ as the divine bridegroom. He shows how Augustine and other commentators understood this relationship:

> So thoroughly was the figure of Christ the Bridegroom
> interinvolved with the concept of Christ the Redeemer,
> that commentators early inaugurated the tradition that
> Christ's words on the cross (*"consummatum est"* in the
> Vulgate, John 19: 30) signified that Christ mounted the
> cross as a bed on which to consummate the marriage with
> humanity inaugurated at the Incarnation, in the supreme
> act of sacrifice which both certified and prefigured His
> apocalyptic marriage at the end of time.
>
> (1971: 45)

This image of Christ mounting the cross as his eschatological
wedding bed is disturbing. Marriage is signified as a sacrificial act,
of which Christ made the ultimate once for all sacrifice (e.g. the
Epistle to the Hebrews). This interpretation by theologians in the
early church eroticizes the death of Jesus. The grotesque terror of
the earthly Crucifixion as the consummating act of history on the
marriage bed of heaven leads to an understanding of martyrdom and
suffering as redemptive and possibly necessary for bodily purity for
the Kingdom. How then is the scream on the cross (Mark 15: 17:
"Then Jesus gave a loud cry and breathed his last") to be inter-
preted? Is this "big death" the consummation of so many (for Jesus,
repressed?) "little deaths"? Is worshipping at the cross a veneration
of the phallus? Such bloodletting on the cross drains the flesh of
impurities so that a more complete transformation, resurrection
may occur. The heavenly marriage act at the Last Judgment can
thus be without stain.

What kinds of transformation are occurring in the virginal males
(Apoc. 14: 4–5) who enter the Bride of Christ and then become her?
Is the heaven of the Apocalypse an all-male domain, or is it a place
of some men transforming into women by violation of the Whore
("Come out of her, my people" in 18: 4), and other men by their
virginal state and status as among the 144,000 and their violation
of the Bride? Also, are women (as part of the great company of the
redeemed in Chapter 7, the souls under the altar in 6: 9, and "my
people" in 18: 4) having sexual relations with the Whore (and with
Jezebel in 2: 22) and eventually becoming men who become women
through sexual acts with women? I do not think Keller is correct
that the Whore is patriarchy in drag, since cities were considered
female in the ancient world. Also, there is no indication in the
Hebrew Bible that Israel as God's wife is a patriarchal country in
drag. In a reversal of some early Christian beliefs that women's

bodies had to become male after death to reach heaven, must the male body in the Apocalypse become female (or at least be in female dress) to dwell with God? Are the 144,000 (and whoever else is saved for this realm) the mass "female" consorts of the male God? Could this be the ultimate of what Jean Genet calls "gender fuck"? – the transgression of every gender boundary and heightening of ambiguities with deities and angels and all the company of heaven? Or perhaps this paradise is "gender rape,"[3] and heaven is the sequel of the rape of the Whore and of the Bride. Is God the grand director and voyeur of this heavenly orgy? Is there role switching in which God and the readers are voyeurs? Does fascination with the throne room represent some of the obsession with the monarchy and the sex lives of the rich, famous and powerful? Are we as readers the paparazzi, chasing down worldly suffering and disasters for a glimpse of the deity and his "coming" apocalypse?

Genet's main character in his book *Our Lady of the Flowers*, Divine, is a male prostitute who plays the passive feminine in sex acts. He deems this queen a saint (Genet 1963: 194; Millett 1969: 344–5). Thus, for Genet the elect are drag queens. Kate Millett reveals that Genet's main statement in his play:

> is that unless the ideology of real or fantasized virility is abandoned, unless the clinging to male supremacy as a birthright is finally foregone, all systems of oppression will continue to function simply by virtue of their logical and emotional mandate in the primary human situation.
>
> (1969: 21)

In other words, unless the idea of a hypermasculine Father God is abandoned, heaven remains a sanitized place where the only role for the female is played by men.

The body of God in the Apocalypse is male. In his provocative study of God as body-builder, Stephen Moore notes that the Son of Man in the Apocalypse has feet of bronze (1: 15), and he links this image with the vision on the bronzed body-builder who is like a bronze statue. For Moore, the God of the Apocalypse is a posing body-builder, an Arnold Schwartzenegger with throne in *Conan the Barbarian* (1996: 121–2). With massive masculinity, like in Conan and Rambo characters, God and the Son of Man leave "mountains of dead bodies... irrefutable proof that the exaggerated majesty of the one seated on the throne is warranted: he can kill at will without lifting a finger – or moving a muscle" (1996: 122).[4] The apocalyptic God is a pin-up hunk, a "man's man" in terms of the text. Is some aspect of this God a male God who is male-identified? God has no female consort, and he is also identified by female metaphors in parts of the Bible. With Moore, I think the Apocalypse has as much to do with theology (gazing on God) as eschatology (gazing on the End). This hunk God directs myriads of angel armies to destroy his creation. This male-bonding experience in heaven is aided by the "war experience," since those who make it to heaven have fought the good fight for God, which in the Apocalypse involves active nonviolent resistance to the forces of evil.

The ultimate bonding of God and men occurs in the divine marriage. Male believers become women/brides in order to dwell for eternity in holy matrimony with the deity. The female church (like the traditional minyan) is all men. The male body identifies with the male God. The male becomes female to unite with God – Eve's trick without Eve, and without God's interference. Lilith and Eve (and Asherah, God's consort) are demonized to make room for the men who become women to unite with God. By becoming women, men can love a man (God) without the threat of homosexuality.[5] Howard Eilberg-Schwartz states, "By imagining men as wives of God, Israelite religion was partially able to preserve the heterosexual complementarity that helped to define the culture" (1994: 3). He adds that "When males wished to know or be known by God, a potentially homoerotic relationship was avoided by feminizing one of the parties involved" (1994: 18). Eden was a place of male and female, a heterosexist place, while at the other end of the Bible the heavenly paradise is a place of gender ambiguity (a transgendered paradise?). Unity at last, but on God's terms. What does reigning with God entail? With no more procreation necessary, are men allowed to cross over the previously defined gender boundaries? According to Bjorn Krondorfer, "A peculiarity in the history of Western Christianity is that it does not worship the *linga* directly but rather divinizes the male body by effeminizing it" (1996: 9). The men in the heavenly throne room are penisless but still retain phallic power.

Does this text bring comfort or disruption to the believer? What of the groups of redeemed outside of the 144,000 that may or may not include women? Whatever the gender make-up of the redeemed groups, God requires the stereotypical passivity of women worshipping at the feet of the master. The redeemed even have the names of Christ and God on their foreheads (Apoc. 14: 1) making them truly slaves of Christ. Is there bondage or freedom in heaven? Heaven is as much a place of terror as hell.[6] Or as the ad for a recent film

Sphere announces, "Terror can fill any space." The "certainties" of heaven include strange transformations and ambiguous sexual boundaries.

Thus, ambiguous sexualities as well as terror fill the throne room of God. Are the Brides of Christ transvestite prostitutes "made good"?[7] Moore points out that the Greek term for "dogs" in the list of outsiders at the end of the Apocalypse can also relate to male prostitutes (1996: 129). Is the Apocalypse engaging in a bit of hypocrisy – male prostitutes of the pagan cults on the outside, but God's special male-brides (male-order brides?) on the inside? The Bride (singular) becomes the excess, Brides (plural).[8] There is the excess of desire, of *jouissance*, of the never-ending story in the Apocalypse. As Genet would say, "Their caricature is grotesque" (Millett 1969: 17). God has more wives than Solomon, whom he condemned. It is not clear in the text whether the marital relationship between God and his brides is sexual or not. J. Michael Clark related to me on this question that "You can go to the gym with God, but you can't sleep with God."[9] In this kinky heaven where sexual acts may or may not occur, there is none the less endless unity with God. This heavenly bliss is postponed, and the reader returns to earth; such bliss is a future hope (?) that will occur after possible suffering. What remains is the terror of the Revelations.

This message is still not liberating for our late twentieth-century feminist and pro-gay liberation movements. Of course, I am using twentieth-century language and terms to define a first-century world view. I make this hermeneutical leap because I want to figure out how to read the Apocalypse in this century of genocide and Aids. In his reading, Eilberg-Schwartz is more positive and finds "various forms of intimate relations to the divine. I find this 'polymorphously perverse theology' extremely liberating" (1994: 242). He sees an opportunity for more diverse ways of identifying with the divine. One might be able to argue from all these ambiguities that God ultimately does not intend male and female in the traditional, gender-sterotyped way we thought. What of the pronouncement at baptism – "there is no longer male and female; for all of you are one in Christ Jesus" (Gal. 3: 28) that makes the believer genderless. Heaven is not genderless, but neither is it gender-bound. What is God doing in this text? God can morph into Son of Man, Lamb, Christ, Spirit, Father, King, Lord God Almighty. The 144,000 change into the Brides. What remains is the misogyny and exclusion by a powerful, wrathful deity. In the Apocalypse, the Kingdom of God is the kingdom of perversity.

Figure 8.2 Detail from *The Calling of the Elect into Heaven* from *The Last Judgment* by Luca Signorelli (*c.* 1450–1523), fresco in the cathedral at Orvieto, Italy

Figure 8.3 Panels from Hans Memling's (*c.* 1430/40–94) *The Last Judgment: The Elect* (left) and *The Damned* (1466–73)

NOTES

PREQUEL, OR PREFACE

1 *Blue Velvet* is especially chilling for me since it was filmed near where I grew up in eastern North Carolina (see chapter 2).
2 According to Keller, "The 144,000 are now physically raised to reign with Christ in a kind of theocratic protectorate" (1996: 79).
3 For example, Jodie Foster's character in *The Silence of the Lambs* and both main characters in *The X-Files* have experienced this unnerving moral soul-searching.
4 I want to thank Jan Tarlin for urging me into confession on these matters.

1 INTRODUCTION: APOCALYPSE AS SEQUEL

1 Žižek summarizes his Lacanian position: "Beautiful, Sublime and Monstrous [*Ungeheure*] form a triad which corresponds to the Lacanian triad of Imaginary, Symbolic and Real.... Beauty makes possible the sublimation of the Monstrous; sublimation mediates between Beautiful and Monstrous; etc." (1997: 218).

2 A GOOD APOCALYPSE IS HARD TO FIND: CROSSING THE APOCALYPTIC BORDERS OF MARK 13

1 This article appeared previously in *Semeia* 72 (1995), special issue, "Taking It Personally," Janice Capel Anderson and Jeffrey L. Staley (eds).

3 JEZEBEL REVAMPED

1 A different version of this article appears in Athalya Brenner, *A Feminist Companion to Samuel and Kings*, Sheffield: Sheffield Academic Press, 1994 and in *Semeia* 69/70 (1995) on "Intertextuality and the Bible," George Aichele and Gary Phillips (eds).

NOTES

2 I conducted an informal survey of college students (ages 18 to 50), Atlanta area artists, and members from both Episcopal and southern Baptist congregations.
3 Emphasis added. On the masculinity of the Jezebel figure, see Patricia Morton (1991: 153): Black women's history:

> has been shaped in the image of Jezebel who deserved what she got because she was other than womanly. And the image of black womanhood as other than womanly has served to confirm black manhood as other than manly, and thus to confirm that the Negro was other and less than fully deserving of racial equality.

In an early twentieth-century drama (McDowall 1924), Jezebel speaks twice of her desire to be male: "Oh, would I were a man that I might go myself with them and face Elijah too" (1924: 12) and "Oh! God! If only I had been a man!" (1924: 21). In film representations the jezebel is termed a "superfemale" as opposed to the more masculine "superwoman." The superfemale is "a woman who, while exceedingly 'feminine' and flirtatious, is too ambitious and intelligent for the docile role society has decreed she play. She is uncomfortable, but not so uncomfortable as to rebel completely; her circumstances are too pleasurable" (Haskell 1987: 214). The film image that comes to mind is Bette Davis in her academy award-winning role in the 1932 Jezebel, in which she plays a southern woman who schemes and destroys those around her and eventually almost destroys herself. In the final scene she rides off toward possible vindication.

Teresa de Lauretis expresses a parallel notion in her feminist critique of Derrida:

> Were I to do so, however, I would earn Derrida's contempt for "those women feminists so derided by Nietzsche," I would put myself in the position of one "who aspires to be like a man," who "seeks to castrate" and "wants a castrated woman".... I shall not do so, therefore. Decency and shame prevent me, though nothing more.
>
> (1987: 47)

4 Elijah is "that much-overestimated 'man of God'" (Stanton 1974: 75). Ellen Battelle Dietrick adds a contemporary note, calling on the reader "to imagine why Jezebel is now [1895] dragged forth to 'shake her gory locks' as a frightful example to the American women who ask for recognized right to self-government" (in Stanton 1974: 75). Are these "gory locks" also an allusion to Medusa – dred/dreaded/dreadful/dred-locks?
5 E.B. Johnston (1982: 1057) finds a word play in Jezebel's name: *zebel* in Jezebel's name is made a pun in 2 Kings 9: 37 with the word "dung" (*domen*).

129

NOTES

6 On the double monster in the mother and daughter relationship see
Gallop (1989). She finds the mother–daughter relationship reflected in
groups of women: "One monster cannot be separated from the other." I
think this idea has interesting implications for the Jezebel–Athaliah
connection; is the narrator of 1–2 Kings presenting us with a pair of
monsters?

7 See chapter 1, "Jezebel and Mammy: The Mythology of Female
Slavery." On p. 46 White states:

> Southerners, therefore, were hardly of one mind concerning
> African-American women. Jezebel was an image as troubling
> as it was convenient and utilitarian.... On the one hand there
> was the woman obsessed with matters of the flesh, on the
> other was the asexual woman. One was carnal, the other
> maternal. One was at heart a slut, the other was deeply reli-
> gious.

Patricia Morton (1991: 10) follows White's argument: "by labeling
the female slave as a Jezebel, the master's sexual abuse was justified by
presenting her as a woman who deserved what she got... by labeling
the slave woman as a sexual animal – not a real woman at all." Morton
adds that the jezebel was scapegoated: "still cast as Jezebel, the black
woman was assigned responsibility for the supposed sins of black as
well as white men" (1991: 33). See also Victoria Bynum (1992: 35 ff.).
In discussing the Jezebel in Apocalypse 2, Elisabeth Schüssler Fiorenza
rightly draws on the southern tradition:

> Like the historical queen Jezebel, she has served in Western
> thought as the archetype of the sexually dangerous woman.
> During the time of slavery, for instance, the image of Jezebel,
> the whore, became the controlling image of black womanhood
> in white, elite, male propaganda.
>
> (1991: 135)

There is no solid evidence of the extent to which the jezebel title
was used to describe these women.

8 Camp is following Alexander Rofe on this point. Peter Ackroyd states
that "Jezebel becomes a type; into her figure is projected in detail the
hostility to what is believed to be alien practice" (1983: 256). Elise
Boulding (1992: 209) adds:

> Foreign women were dangerous role models for Israelite
> women, with their political ways and priestess notions. We
> shall see the same scenario played out again 1,000 years later,
> in the Christian church fathers' distrust of pagan women and

their priestess tradition. The sexual seduction aspect of this struggle is, I suspect, a male rationalization.

9 The Index of Christian Art at Princeton University lists about twenty respresentations of Jezebel up to 1400 CE. Of these there are approximately ten portraits; the rest are from three scenes of her life.
10 Bram Dijkstra refers to "the dead woman as object of desire" in his work on nineteenth- to twentieth-century iconography of evil women (1986: 51).
11 Robbins's protagonist Ellen Cherry considers Jezebel "her doppelgänger." He describes her search for the biblical Jezebel:

> she had procured a bible and gone searching for the lurid details of Jezebel's debauchery. From Sunday school, she had a hazy picture of a thoroughly immoral harlot who costumed herself like a rock 'n' roll vamp, but she couldn't recall a single biographical fact. Imagine her surprise when the Old Testament Book of Kings informed her that Jezebel was a royal – and faithful – wife.
>
> (1990: 32)

12 Thibault defines social semiotics as a theory that moves semiotics "beyond its self-identification with many of the foundational ideological assumptions of Western culture" (1991: 3). Social semiotics is connected with social heteroglossia as follows:

> The systems of voices in the social semiotic, including potentially unvoiced meanings and practices, comprise the relations of social heteroglossia through which relations of alliance, consensus, opposition, conflict, and co-optation among voices are positioned and articulated in specific texts and intertextual formations.
>
> (1991: 25)

Morgan (1985: 8) relates this point: "Indeed, *culture* itself, or the collection of signifying practices in a society, *is radically intertextual.*" On the materiality of language see Kristeva (1975).
13 An older woman student of mine recently commented that Jezebel is that (or any) evil woman who steals husbands. Then she added with a wink, "There's a part of Jezebel in me."

4 THE POWER OF BABEL: SPIRALING OUT OF CONTROL

1 In a conversation with Jan Botha he pointed out that in apartheid South Africa both Genesis 11 and Acts 2 were an argument for the separation of the races. The unity of the tower was a sin; God brought it down; Pentecost is about different languages and separate peoples.

2 Saddam Hussein also has been imposing his name on stones of ancient buildings of Babylon; see Jehl (1997: 4).

3 In terms of Babel and Pentecost, Baudrillard has an interesting thought that might highlight the differences: "radical exoticism versus the pimping of differences" (1993: 147). Is Peter the primary pimp as head of the Church? Along with "ethics after Babel" is needed an "ethics after Pentecost."

4 See chapter 7 in Grosz (1995) for a lengthy discussion of chora with Plato, Derrida, and Irigaray.

5 PEERING INTO THE ABYSS: A POSTMODERN READING OF THE BIBLICAL BOTTOMLESS PIT

1 This article appeared previously in *The New Literary Criticism and the New Testament*, Elizabeth Struthers Malbon and Edgar V. McKnight (eds), Sheffield: Sheffield Academic Press, 1994.

2 For a discussion of maps working in a society "as a form of power-knowledge," see J.B. Harley's (1992) article on deconstructing geography.

3 Northrop Frye defines "prison-house" from Wordsworth as a descent theme from the innocent state of birth into a state "of corruption or confusion" (1976: 100).

4 Most of these basic definitions can be found in Bible dictionaries; see Jeremias for a brief discussion of the idea of the abyss as a spirit prison (1964: 10).

5 See also the discussion in Pippin (1993).

6 Michael Goldberg states that medieval representations of the hell mouth come from the Isaiah 5: 14 image of a large, wide open, mouth. He cites "the Psalter of St. Swithin's Priory, the famous York Minster Mouth of Hell" and Tennyson's *Charge of the Light Brigade*: "Into the mouth of hell / Rode the six hundred" (1992: 342).

7 In the Shepherd of Hermas' Vision 4: I fiery locusts come out of the mouth of the beast "like some Leviathan" (Reddish 1990: 258).

8 Leonard Thompson notes, "Abaddon parallels death, the grave, and Sheol" (1990: 220, n. 11).

9 The idea of pain is expressed in Korean Minjung theology. A. Sung Park defines Han as "the boiled-down feeling of pain caused by injustice and oppression. It is the deep-seated lamentation or bitterness of the suffering Minjung" (1989: 50). And, "Han is the abyss of grief which is deeply embedded in the collective unconscious history of the Korean Minjung" (1989: 51). As the abyss of pain, Han is a text of pain in Korean liberation hermeneutics.

10 Paul Ricoeur focuses on the creation of evil in the *Enuma Elish*: "If the divine came into being, then chaos is anterior to order and the principle of evil is primordial, coextensive with the generation of the divine." Of Tiamat and Apsu representing the waters of the earth, Ricoeur adds, "But this liquid chaos has a surcharge of meaning, in which the myth of the origin of evil takes shape. For Tiamat is more

than the visible immensity of the waters; she has the power to produce" (1967: 177).

E.M. Cioran also focuses on the productive power of the abyss, not on evil but of creative possibility: "Let us return to the original chaos!... Let our being tremble with effort and madness in the fiery abyss!... The disintegration of the world is creation in reverse: an apocalypse upside down but sprung from similar impulses." For Cioran, facing the Infinite is terrifying and joyful all at once. The sense of existential despair over apocalypse is treated by entering the creative chaos: "In every whirlwind hides a potential for form, just as in chaos there is a potential cosmos.... I can only live at the beginning or the end of this world" (1992: 90).

11 Dudley Young examines the mythological roots of chaos as "the yawning womb-tomb abyss from which Mother Earth arose to deliver the cosmos" and as "a deathly hole just waiting to grab the inattentive or unlucky" (1991: 182).

12 Hayles lists some recent films to illustrate the point of a "false future": "*Back to the Future, Brazil, Terminator {I, II},* and *Peggy Sue Got Married*" (1990: 280).

13 Jane Gallop adds in her discussion of male castration desire: "Desire shall henceforth be wed to castration because the phallic signifier is the mark of desire" (1989: 145).

14 Hélène Cixous also criticizes Lacan's phallocentric focus or "phallogo-centric sublation." The male myth is that women are between "two horrifying myths: between the Medusa and the abyss" (1991: 341).

15 Thompson reveals the function of controlling the abyss: "Through images of locks, keys, chains, seals, loosing, and binding John is able to describe controlled movement between earth and Hades (1990: 1, 20: 1–3). Since the realm below represents not only the demonic but also death, movement to and from that realm may also occur in the form of transformation from death to life, or resurrection" (1990: 83).

16 In Eastern religions such as Buddhism and Hinduism, the concept of nothingness (or *sunyata*, emptiness) is positive and represents freedom.

17 John Caputo asserts that Derrida's understanding of absence is an absence of signs. He states:

> Is not the *sur-prise* [of Rousseau] the way we are taken-in, or drawn-out, by the movement of with-drawal?... Is not this play the play of Being, of the abyss, the world-play which plays without why across the epochs?... Instead of the substitute, Derrida should speak of the aboriginal abyss; instead of the supplement, the hidden depths; instead of masturbation, the primal birth of things in *lethe.*
>
> (1985: 199)

18 One common theme in millenarian thought is that of television as the hell mouth (Boyer 1993: 237).

6 APOCALYPTIC HORROR

1 This article appeared in a different form in a special issue on "Fantasy and the Bible" for the *Journal of the Fantastic in the Arts* 8/2 (1997), Tina Pippin and George Aichele (eds).

2 See the discussion of the uncanny as female (especially the womb and the home) in horror films in Creed (1993: 53–8). Barbara Johnson comments on the destruction of Frankenstein's female monster, "the home can be the very site of the *unheimlich*" (1987: 66).

3 The criterion of fear comes from H.P. Lovecraft (Todorov 1973: 32).

4 See the summary in *The Penguin Encyclopedia of Horror and the Supernatural* (Sullivan 1986: 409–11).

5 Carroll shows that for Kant, "disgust stands in the way of the sublime" (1990: 240, n. 20).

6 On the focus of the abject on the female in the Apocalypse – Jezebel, the Woman Clothed with the Sun, the Whore of Babylon, and the Bride of Christ – see Pippin (1992).

7 Carroll relates a variety of emotional responses to horror: "muscular contractions, tension, cringing, shrinking, shuddering, recoiling, tingling, frozenness, momentary arrests, chilling (hence, 'spine-chilling'), paralysis, trembling, nausea, a reflex of apprehension or physically heightened alertness (a danger response), perhaps involuntary screaming, and so on" (1990: 24).

8 Stephen King elaborates on his feelings of writing *The Stand*: "the big battle was not for gasoline allocations but for human souls. There was a feeling – I must admit it – that I was doing a fast, happy tapdance on the grave of the whole world" (1983: 400).

9 Many horror theorists do not find the concept of catharsis helpful for understanding horror texts. Stephen King finds some use for the term:

> The term *catharsis* is as old as Greek drama, and it has been used rather too glibly by some practitioners in my field to justify what they do, but it still has its limited uses here. The dream of horror is in itself an out-letting and a lancing… and it may well be that the mass-media dream of horror can sometimes become a nationwide analyst's couch.
>
> (1983: 13)

Grixti notes: "Arguments about the need for 'cathartic release' of aggressive impulses have frequently been used to justify some very disturbing fictional and not-so fictional elaborations of sadistic violence" (1989: 106).

10 Carroll notes that the massing of creatures increases their horror effect:

> As with the case of magnification, with massification it is not the case that any kind of entity can be grouped into horrific hordes. It must be the sort of thing we are already prone to

find repellent... by augmenting the threat posed by these antecedently phobic objects.

(1990: 50)

11 For a discussion of the cruelty theme see Hallie (1969: 165).

12 On the topic of monstrous births traced to women, see Huet (1993: 6): "Monstrous births were understood as warnings and public testimony; they were thought to be 'demonstrations' of the mother's unfulfilled desires." Huet's study is of monstrous births in the Renaissance as traceable to the mother's "unspoken bestial desire" (1993: 21). She finds the root meaning of monster as "warning" and "demonstrate" in the way that "monsters were signs sent by God" (1993: 6). The Apocalypse has both male and female monsters; unlike Dr Frankenstein in Mary Shelley's book, the Apocalypse is able to create female monsters.

13 Schlobin also says about the text of Job as horror literature:

Job's story may be the most soul-chilling of all time; no wonder so many have placed intellectual balms on its piercing darkness. Moreover, its deadly fangs have been all the greater since it is set within accompanying literature that lulls unsuspecting readers into false expectations of comfort and healing.

(1992: 35)

Has scholarship on the Apocalypse also created such "false expectations" of this text as a text of "comfort and healing"?

14 David Blumenthal deals with the abusiveness of God by dealing with the difficult passages directly. He states:

Abusive behaviour is abusive; it is inexcusable, in all circumstances.... Our sins – and we are always sinful – are in no proportion whatsoever to the punishment meted out to us.... To have faith in a post-holocaust, abuse-sensitive world is, first, to know – to recognize and to admit – that God is an abusing God, but not always.

(1993: 248)

15 Paul Boyer (1992) makes an excellent case for the historical linking of conservative Christianity and conservative (right-wing) politics. In a psychological study of belief in the Apocalypse, Charles Strozier calls the symptom "endism," and argues that "the location of self in some future, ultimate narrative, pushes such reflection into a profoundly different realm, wrapping the future in magical projections that isolate it from meaningful, human connection with the past" (1994: 1). Endism holds to the violent ending of the world; one can avoid being in the violent end by being written in the book of life. Susan Sontag relates a similar idea: "A pseudo-familiarity with the horrible reinforces alienation, making one less able to react in real life" (quoted in Skal 1993: 22).

7 APOCALYPTIC FEAR

1 See Jean Delumeau's study of sin and fear in Western culture. He maintains that for Protestant preachers in the eighteenth century, "the fear of God is the foundation of all religion.... [F]aith produces fear and fear confirms faith. Love without fear becomes irreverent, and fear without love becomes anguished. Fear authorizes joy, and joy sweetens fear, making it pleasing and delicious" (1991: 503).

2 Pinedo relates, "In postmodern horror film either the monster triumphs or the outcome is uncertain" (1997: 31). Classic horror films work on the following premise: "The monster is destroyed and the normative order restored" (1997: 30).

8 CONCLUSION: THE JOY OF (APOCALYPTIC) SEX

1 Adela Yarbro Collins believes that the scene of the Whore of Babylon is not about sexual desire (biblical interpretation article).

2 Jameson was a respondent to papers at the 1990 Society of Biblical Literature Ideological Criticism Consultation; see *Semeia* 59 (1992).

3 I owe this comment to Jan Tarlin.

4 Moore also argues that in the Apocalypse the Roman Emperor Domitian becomes a god, and becomes Yahweh; in other words, Yahweh is a divinized Domitian (1996: 134). Although the God of the Apocalypse is a military ruler like Domitian and all other Roman emperors, the slippery date of the Apocalypse leaves this an open question – a nonexact image. I find it odd that Moore resorts to mainstream historical-critical readings of the Apocalypse; is this reading strategy a protection against the sublime horror of the text?

5 In a section called, "Apocalyptics of the Closet," Mary Wilson Carpenter notes that "The 'key' image of apocalyptic marriage is indeed a keystone of male homosocial desire, articulating the incorporation of the feminine with the evacuation of the female body, complying with compulsory heterosexuality but celebrating a union with 'nature'" (1995: 124). I think the issue is more complex than strictly defined male and female bodies. Carpenter also fails to investigate further any readings of the gender ambiguities of the Apocalypse and chooses instead to focus on the failure of biblical scholars to acknowledge the gender violence specifically on females in the text. In her limited research, she assumes no biblical scholars have made this point.

6 In a section called, "Heaven Can Be Hell," Moore rightly calls the heaven of the Apocalypse "a Foucauldian nightmare" of the "inner self-policing" by the believer (1996: 128).

7 Does God know these are men in drag? Or is this another situation like in the film *The Crying Game*? Of course, the tradition is that the omniscient God would know all, and that is also disturbing.

8 In medieval theology the soul is imagined as a bride/queen enthroned with Christ (see McDannell and Lang 1988: 104).

9 Personal conversation.

BIBLIOGRAPHY

Abrams, M.H. (1971) *Natural Supernaturalism: Tradition and Revolution in Romantic Literature*, New York: W.W. Norton.

Achtemeier, Paul J. (ed.) (1985) *Harper's Bible Dictionary*, San Francisco: HarperSanFrancisco.

Ackroyd, Peter R. (1985) "Goddesses, Women and Jezebel," in Averil Cameron and Amelie Kuhrt (eds) *Images of Women in Antiquity*, Detroit, MI: Wayne State University Press.

Allen, Virginia (1983) *The Femme Fatale Erotic Icon*, Troy, NY: Whitson.

Althusser, Louis (1994) "Ideology and Ideological Sate Apparatuses (Notes Towards an Investigation)," in Slavoj Žižek (ed.) *Mapping Ideology*, London: Verso.

Altizer, Thomas J.J. (1990) *Genesis and Apocalypse: A Theological Voyage Toward Authentic Christianity*, Louisville, KY: Westminster/John Knox Press.

American Heritage Dictionary (1997) 3rd edn, Boston, MA: Houghton Mifflin.

Anderson, Laurie (1995) "The End of the World," in *The Ugly One Wears the Jewels*, Warner Bros. Records.

Ashley, Kathleen, Leigh Gilmore, and Gerald Peters (eds) (1994) *Autobiography and Postmodernism*, Amherst: University of Massachusetts Press.

Atheker, Bettina (1989) *Tapestries of Life: Women's Work, Women's Consciousness, and the Meaning of Daily Experience*, Amherst: University of Massachusetts Press.

Atwood, Margaret (1984) *The Edible Woman*, New York: Bantam.

Bachelard, Gaston (1969) *The Poetics of Space*, trans. Maria Jolas, Boston, MA: Beacon Press.

Bal, Mieke (1987) *Lethal Love: Feminist Literary Readings of Biblical Love Stories*, Bloomington: Indiana University Press.

—— (1988) *Death and Dissymmetry: The Politics of Coherence in the Book of Judges*, Chicago, IL: University of Chicago Press.

—— (1991) *Reading "Rembrandt": Beyond the Word–Image Opposition*, New York: Cambridge University Press.

Barazun, Jacques (1986) "Romanticism," in Jacques Barazun (ed.) *The Penguin Encyclopedia of Horror and the Supernatural*, New York: Viking.

—— (1986) "Introduction," in Jacques Barazun (ed.), *The Penguin Encyclopedia of Horror and the Supernatural*, New York: Viking.

Barbor, H.R. (n.d.) *Jezebel: A Tragedy in Three Acts*, London: Arthur Brenton.

Barkey, Jeanne (1983) untitled article, *off our backs* 2: 1.

Barnard, P. Mordaunt (1904) *Jezebel: A Drama*, London: Francis Griffiths.

Barnes, Trevor J. and James S. Duncan (1992) "Introduction: Writing Worlds," in Trevor J. Barnes and James S. Duncan (eds) *Writing Worlds: Discourse, Text and Metaphor in the Representation of Landscape*, London/New York: Routledge.

Barr, Marleen S. (1992) *Feminist Fabulation: Space/Postmodern Fiction*, Iowa City: University of Iowa Press.

Barthes, Roland (1977) "The Death of the Author," in *Image, Music, Text*, trans. S. Heath, New York: Hill & Wang.

Bartkowski, Frances (1989) *Feminist Utopias*, Lincoln: University of Nebraska Press.

Bataille, Georges (1973) *Literature and Evil*, London: Calder & Boyars.

—— (1985) *Visions of Excess: Selected Writings, 1927–1939*, ed. Allan Stoekl and trans. Allan Stoekl with Carl R. Lovitt and Donald M. Leslie, Jr, Minneapolis: University of Minnesota Press.

—— (1986) *Eroticism: Death and Sensuality*, trans. Mary Dalwood, San Francisco, CA: City Lights Books.

—— (1989) *The Tears of Eros*, trans. Peter Connor, San Francisco, CA: City Lights Books.

Baudrillard, Jean (1989) "The Anorexic Ruins," in Dietmar Kamper and Christoph Wulf (eds) *Looking Back on the End of the World*, trans. David Antal, New York: Semiotext(e).

—— (1993) *The Transparency of Evil: Essays on Extreme Phenomena*, trans. James Benedict, London: Verso.

—— (1997) "Hysteresis of the Millennium," in Charles B. Stozier and Michael Flynn (eds) *The Year 2000: Essays on the End*, New York: New York University Press.

Benítez-Rojo, Antonio (1992) *The Repeating Island: The Caribbean and the Postmodern Perspective*, Durham, NC: Duke University Press.

Benstock, Shari (ed.) (1988) *The Private Self: Theory and Practice of Women's Autobiographical Writings*, Chapel Hill: University of North Carolina Press.

Berry, Philippa and Andrew Wernick (eds) (1992) *Shadow of Spirit: Postmodernism and Religion*, London/New York: Routledge.

Best, Sue (1995) "Sexualizing Space," in Elizabeth Grosz and Elspeth Probyn (eds) *Sexy Bodies: The Strange Carnalities of Feminism*, London/New York: Routledge.

Blanchot, Maurice (1986) *The Writing of the Disaster*, trans. Ann Smock, Lincoln: University of Nebraska Press.

—— (1992) *The Step Not Beyond*, trans. Lycette Nelson, Albany: State University of New York Press.

Bloom, Harold and David Rosenberg (1990) *The Book of J*, New York: Grove Weidenfeld.

Blumenthal, David (1993) *Facing the Abusing God: A Theology of Protest*, Louisville, KY: Westminster/John Knox Press.

Bost, Hubert (1985) *Babel: du texte au symbole*, Genève: Labor et Fides.

Bottigheimer, Ruth B. (1996) *The Bible for Children: From the Age of Gutenberg to the Present*, New Haven, CT: Yale University Press.

Boulding, Elise (1992) *The Underside of History: A View of Women through Time*, vol. 1, revised edition, Newbury Park, CA: Sage.

Boyer, Paul (1992) *When Time Shall Be No More: Prophecy Belief in Modern American Culture*, Cambridge, MA: Harvard University Press.

Brodzki, Bella and Celeste Schenck (eds) (1988) *Life/Lines: Theorizing Women's Autobiography*, Ithaca, NY: Cornell University Press.

Bronfen, Elisabeth (1992) *Over Her Dead Body: Death, Femininity and the Aesthetic*, London/New York: Routledge.

Brooke-Rose, Christine (1981) *A Rhetoric of the Unreal: Studies in Narative and Structure, Especially of the Fantastic*, New York: Cambridge University Press.

Brooks, Peter (1993) *Body Work: Objects of Desire in Modern Narrative*, Cambridge, MA: Harvard University Press.

Brophy, Philip (1986) "Horrality: The Textuality of Contemporary Horror Films," *Screen* 27(1): 2–13.

Bulkin, Elly, Minne Bruce Pratt, and Barbara Smith (1984) *Yours in the Struggle: Three Perspectives on Anti-Semitism and Racism*, New York: Long Haul.

Butler, Judith (1993) *Bodies that Matter: On the Discursive Limits of "Sex,"* London/New York: Routledge.

Bynum, Caroline Walker (1995) *The Resurrection of the Body in Western Christianity, 200–1336*, New York: Columbia University Press.

Bynum, Victoria E. (1992) *Unruly Women: The Politics of Social and Sexual Control in the Old South*, Chapel Hill: The University of North Carolina Press.

Camp, Claudia V. (1992) "1 and 2 Kings," in Carol A. Newsom and Sharon H. Ringe (eds) *The Women's Bible Commentary*, Louisville, KY: Westminster/John Knox.

Campbell, Will D. (1977) *Brother to a Dragonfly*, New York: Seabury Press.

—— (1986) *Forty Acres and a Goat*, Atlanta, GA: Peachtree Publishers.

Caputo, John D. (1985) "From the Primordiality of Absence to the Absence of Primordiality: Heidegger's Critique of Derrida," in Hugh J. Silverman and Don Ihde (eds) *Hermeneutics and Deconstruction*, Albany: State University of New York Press.

—— (1997) *The Prayers and Tears of Jacques Derrida: Religion without Religion*, Bloomington: Indiana University Press.

Carpenter, Mary Wilson (1995) "Representing Apocalypse: Sexual Politics and the Violence of Revelation," in Richard Dellamora (ed.) *Postmodern Apocalypse: Theory and Cultural Practice at the End*, Philadelphia: University of Pennsylvania Press.

Carroll, Noël (1990) *The Philosophy of Horror or Paradoxes of the Heart*, London/New York: Routledge.

Carter, Chris (1993-8) *The X-Files*, Fox Network.

Chambers, Ross (1990) "Alter Ego: Intertextuality, Irony and the Politics of Reading," in Michael Worton and Judith Still (eds) *Intertextuality: Theories and Practices*, Manchester: Manchester University Press.

Chisholm, Dianne (1995) "The 'Cunning Lingua' of Desire," in Elizabeth Grosz and Elspeth Probyn (eds) *Sexy Bodies: The Strange Carnalities of Feminism*, London/New York: Routledge.

Cioran, E.M. (1996) *On the Heights of Despair*, trans. Ilinca Zarifopal-Johnston, Berkeley: University of California Press.

Cixous, Hélène (1991) "The Laugh of the Medusa," in Robyn R. Warhol and Diane Price Herndl (eds) *Feminisms: An Anthology of Literary Theory and Criticism*, New Brunswick, NJ: Rutgers University Press.

Clayton, Jay (1993) *The Pleasures of Babel: Contemporary American Literature and Theory*, New York: Oxford University Press.

Clifford, James and George E. Marcus (eds) (1986) *Writing Culture: The Poetics and Politics of Ethnography*, Berkeley: University of California Press.

Cohn, Norman (1993) *Cosmos, Chaos and the World to Come: The Ancient Roots of Apocalyptic Faith*, New Haven, CT: Yale University Press.

Collins, Adela Yarbro (1984) *Crisis and Catharsis: The Power of the Apocalypse*, Philadelphia, PA: The Westminster Press.

Collins, John J. (1997) *Apocalypticism in the Dead Sea Scrolls*, London/New York: Routledge.

Cooper, J.C. (1978) *An Illustrated Encyclopedia of Traditional Symbols*, London: Thames & Hudson.

Craven, Wes (dir.) (1994) *Wes Craven's New Nightmare*, New Line Cinema.

—— (1997) *Scream 2*, New Line Cinema.

Creed, Barbara (1993) *The Monstrous-Feminine: Film. Feminism, Psychoanalysis*, London/New York: Routledge.

Culver, R.D. (1975) "Jezebel," in *The Zondervan Pictorial Encyclopedia*, vol. 3, Grand Rapids, MI: Merrill C. Tenney.

Daly, Mary (1978) *Gyn/Ecology: The Metaethics of Radical Feminism*, Boston, MA: Beacon.

Davidson, Clifford and Thomas H. Seiler (eds) (1992) *The Iconography of Hell*, Kalamazoo: Medieval Institute Publications.

de Lauretis, Teresa (ed.) (1986) *Feminist Studies/Critical Studies*, Bloomington: Indiana University Press.

—— (1987) *Technologies of Gender: Essays on Theory, Film and Fiction*, Bloomington: Indiana University Press.

Dellamora, Richard (1994) *Apocalyptic Overtures: Sexual Politics and the Sense of an Ending*, New Brunswick, NJ: Rutgers University Press.

—— (1995) *Postmodern Apocalypse: Theory and Cultural Practice at the End*, Philadelphia, University of Pennsylvania Press.

Delumeau, Jean (1991) *Sin and Fear: The Emergence of Western Guilt Culture, 13th–18th Centuries*, trans. Eric Nicholson, New York: St Martin's Press.

de Man, Paul (1979) "Autobiography as Defacement," *Modern Language Notes* 94: 919–30.

Derrida, Jacques (1974) *Of Grammatology*, trans. Gayatri Chakravorty Spivak, Baltimore, MD: The Johns Hopkins University Press.

—— (1979) *Spurs: Nietzsche's Styles*, trans. Barbara Harlow, Chicago, IL: University of Chicago Press.

—— (1981) *Dissemination*, trans. Barbara Johnson, Chicago, IL: University of Chicago Press.

—— (1982) "Of an Apocalyptic Tone Recently Adopted in Philosophy," trans. John P. Leavey, *Semeia* 23: 63–97.

—— (1984) "No Apocalypse, Not Now (Full Speed Ahead, Seven Missiles, Seven Missives)," *Diacritics* 14: 20-1.

—— (1985) *The Ear of the Other: Otobiography, Transference, Translation*, ed. Christie V. MacDonald, trans. Peggy Kamuf, New York: Schocken Books.

—— (1993) "On a Newly Arisen Apocalyptic Tone in Philosophy," in Peter Fenves (ed.) *Raising the Tone of Philosophy: Late Essays by Immanuel Kant, Transformative Justice by Jacques Derrida*, trans. John Leavey, Jr, Baltimore, MD: Johns Hopkins University Press.

Detweiler, Robert (1989) *Breaking the Fall: Religious Readings of Contemporary Fiction*, San Francisco: Harper & Row.

Diamond, Arlyn and Lee Edwards (eds) (1977) *The Authority of Experience*, Amherst: University of Massachusetts Press.

Dijkstra, Bram (1986) *Idols of Perversity: Fantasies of Feminine Evil in Fin-de-Siècle Culture*, New York: Oxford University Press.

—— (1996) *Evil Sisters: The Threat of Female Sexuality in Twentieth-Century Culture*, New York: Henry Holt.

Doane, Mary Ann (1988) "Women's Stake: Filming the Female Body," in Constance Penley (ed.) *Feminism and Film Theory*, London/New York: Routledge.

Donaldson, Laura E. (1992) *Decolonizing Feminisms: Race, Gender, and Empire Building*, Chapel Hill: University of North Carolina Press.

Dworkin, Andrea (1983) *Right-wing Women*, New York: Pedigree Books.

Eakin, Paul John (1985) *Fictions in Autobiography: Studies in the Art of Self-Invention*, Princeton, NJ: Princeton University Press.

Eco, Umberto (1995) *The Search for the Perfect Language*, trans. James Fentress, Cambridge: Blackwell.

Eilberg-Schwartz, Howard (1994) *God's Phallus and Other Problems for Men and Monotheism*, Boston, MA: Beacon Press.

Enright, D.J. (ed.) (1995) *The Oxford Book of the Supernatural*, New York: Oxford University Press.

Exum, Cheryl (1985) "Jezebel," in Paul J. Achtemeier (ed.) *Harper's Bible Dictionary*, San Francisco, CA: Harper & Row.

Fabian, Cosi (1997) "The Holy Whore: A Woman's Gateway to Power," in Jill Nagle (ed.) *Whores and Other Feminists*, New York: Routledge.

Feldman, Susan (ed.) (1963) *African Myths and Tales*, New York: Dell Publishing Company.

Finn, Robin (1997) "Despite Its Charms, Horror Can Pale," *The New York Times*, January 3: B1 and B22.

Forshey, Gerald E. (1992) *American Religious and Biblical Spectaculars*, New York: Praeger.

Fowler, Robert (1991) *Let the Reader Understand: Reader-Response Criticism and the Gospel of Mark*, Minneapolis, MN: Fortress Press.

Freud, Sigmund (1958) "The Uncanny," in *On Creativity and the Unconscious*, New York: Harper & Row.

Frow, John (1990) "Intertextuality and Ontology," in Michael Worton and Judith Still (eds) *Intertextuality: Theories and Practices*, Manchester: Manchester University Press.

Frye, Northrop (1976) *The Secular Scripture: A Study of the Structure of Romance*, Cambridge, MA: Harvard University Press.

Funk, Robert, Roy W. Hoover, and the Jesus Seminar (1993) *The Five Gospels: The Search for the Authentic Words of Jesus*, New York: Polebridge Press/Macmillan Publishing Company.

Gallop, Jane (1985) *Reading Lacan*, Ithaca, NY: Cornell University Press.

—— (1989) "The Monster in the Mirror: The Feminist Critic's Psychoanalysis," in Richard Feldstein and Judith Roof (eds) *Feminism and Psychoanalysis*, Ithaca, NY: Cornell University Press.

Game, Ann (1991) *Undoing the Social: Towards a Deconstructive Sociology*, Toronto: University of Toronto Press.

Gassen, Richard W. and Bernhard Holeczek (1985) *Apokalypse: Ein Prinzip Hoffnung? Ernst Bloch zum 100. Geburtstag*, Heidelberg: Edition Braus.

Gebauer, Gunter (1989) "The Place of Beginning and End: Caves and Their Systems of Symbols," in Dietmar Kamper and Christoph Wulf (eds) *Looking Back on the End of the World*, New York: Semiotext(e).

Geddert, Timothy J. (1989) *Watchwords: Mark 13 in Markan Eschatology*, Journal for the Study of the Old Testament 26, Sheffield: Sheffield Academic Press.

Gehman, Henry Snyder (ed.) (1970) *The New Westminster Dictionary of the Bible*, Philadelphia, PA: The Westminster Press.

Genet, Jean (1963) *Our Lady of the Flowers*, trans. Bernard Frechtman, New York: Grove Press.

Gilman, Charlotte Perkins (1979) *Herland: A Lost Feminist Utopian Novel*, New York: Pantheon Books.

Gilmore, Leigh (1994a) *Autobiographics: A Feminist Theory of Women's Self-Representation*, Ithaca, NY: Cornell University Press.

—— (1994b) "The Mark of Autobiography: Postmodernism, Autobiography, and Genre," in Kathleen Ashley, Leigh Gilmore, and Gerald Peters (eds) *Autobiography and Postmodernism*, Amherst: University of Massachusetts Press.

Gleick, James (1987) *Chaos: Making A New Science*, New York: Viking Penguin.

Goldberg, Michael (1992) "Hell," in David Lyle Jeffrey (ed.) *A Dictionary of Biblical Tradition in English Literature*, Grand Rapids, MN: Wm. B. Eerdmans.

Gould, Stephen J. (1997) *Questioning the Apocalypse: A Rationalist's Guide to a Precisely Arbitrary Countdown*, New York: Harmony Books.

Graham, Dan (1993) *Rock My Religion: Writings and Art Projects 1965–1990*, Boston, MA: MIT Press.

Gramsci, Antonio (1971) *Selections from the Prison Notebooks*, ed. and trans. Quintin Hoare and Geoffrey Nowell Smith, New York: International Publishers.

Griffith, D.W. (1916) *Intolerance*, Triangle Productions (film).

Grixti, Joseph (1989) *Terrors of Uncertainty: The Cultural Contexts of Horror Fiction*, London/New York: Routledge.

Grosz, Elizabeth (1990) *Jacques Lacan: A Feminist Introduction,* London/New York: Routledge.

—— (1995) *Space, Time, and Perversion: Essays on the Politics of Bodies*, London/New York: Routledge.

Grosz, Elizabeth and Elspeth Probyn (eds) (1995) *Sexy Bodies: The Strange Carnalities of Feminism*, London/New York: Routledge.

Grubb, Nancy (1997) *Revelations: Art of the Apocalypse*, New York: Abbeville Press.

Gunn, Janet Varner (1982) *Autobiography: Toward a Poetics of Experience*, Philadelphia, PA: University of Pennsylvania Press.

Halberstam, Judith (1995) *Skin Shows: Gothic Horror and the Technology of Monsters*, Durham, NC: Duke University Press.

Hallie, Philip (1969) *The Paradox of Cruelty*, Middletown, CT: Wesleyan University Press.

Hansen, Miriam (1991) *Babel and Babylon: Spectatorship in American Silent Film*, Cambridge, MA: Harvard University Press.

Haraway, Donna J. (1991) *Simians, Cyborgs, and Women: The Reinvention of Nature*, London/New York: Routledge.

—— (1997) *Modest_Witness@Second_Millennium.FemaleMan_Meets_ OncoMouse: Feminism and Technoscience*, London/New York: Routledge.

Harjo, Joy (1983) "I Give You Back," in *She Had Some Horses*, New York: Thunder's Mouth Press.

Harley, J.B. (1992) "Deconstructing the Map," in Trevor J. Barnes and James S. Duncan (eds) *Writing Worlds: Discourse, Text and Metaphor in the Representation of Landscape*, London/New York: Routledge.

Harlow, Barbara (1987) *Resistance Literature*, New York: Methuen.

Hartwell, David G. (ed.) (1992) "Introduction," in David G. Hartwell (ed.) *Foundations of Fear*, New York: Tom Doherty Associates.

Haskell, Molly (1987) *From Reverence to Rape: The Treatment of Women in the Movies*, Chicago, IL: University of Chicago Press.

Hassan, Ihab (1987) *The Postmodern Turn: Essays in Postmodern Theory and Culture*, Columbus: Ohio State University Press.

Hayles, N. Katherine (1990) *Chaos Bound: Orderly Disorder in Contemporary Literature and Science*, Ithaca, NY: Cornell University Press.

Hays, Richard B. (1996) *The Moral Vision of the New Testament: A Contemporary Introduction to New Testament Ethics*, San Francisco, CA: HarperSanFrancisco.

Heller, Terry (1987) *The Delights of Terror: An Aesthetics of the Tale of Terror*, Urbana, IL: University of Illinois Press.

Hemer, Colin J. (1986) *The Letters to the Seven Churches of Asia in their Local Setting*, Sheffield: Journal for the Study of the New Testament.

Herodotus (1920) *Herodotus*, Book I, trans. A.D. Godley, Cambridge, MA: Harvard University Press.

Hillman, James (1987) "Wars, Arms, Rams, Mars: On the Love of War," in Valerie Andrews, Robert Bosnak, and Karen Walter Goodwin (eds) *Facing Apocalypse*, Dallas, TX: Spring Publications.

Hoblit, Gregory (dir.) (1998) *Fallen*, Warner Brothers.

Huber, Paul (1989) *Apokalypse: Bilderzyklen zur Johannes-Offenbarung in Trier, auf dem Athos und von Caillaud d'Angers*, Düsseldorf: Patmos.

Huet, Marie-Hélène (1993) *Monstrous Imagination*, Cambridge, MA: Harvard University Press.

Hunt, Lynn (ed.) (1993) *The Invention of Pornography: Obscenity and the Origins of Modernity, 1500–1800*, New York: Zone Books.

Hutcheon, Linda (1988) *A Poetics of Postmodernism: History, Theory, Fiction*, London/New York: Routledge.

Ingebretsen, Edward J. (1996) *Maps of Heaven, Maps of Hell: Religious Terror as Memory from the Puritans to Stephen King*, Armonk, NY: M.E. Sharpe.

Irigaray, Luce (1985) *This Sex Which Is Not One*, trans. Catherine Porter with Carolyn Burke, Ithaca, NY: Cornell University Press.

—— (1992) *Elemental Passions*, trans. Joanne Collie and Judith Still, London/New York: Routledge.

Jabès, Edmond (1993) *The Book of Margins*, trans. Rosmarie Waldrop, Chicago, IL: University of Chicago Press.

Jackson, Rosemary (1981) *Fantasy: The Literature of Subversion*, New York: Methuen.

Jameson, Fredric (1972) *The Prison-House of Language: A Critical Account of Structuralism and Russian Formalism*, Princeton, NJ: Princeton University Press.

—— (1991) *Postmodernism, or, The Cultural Logic of Late Capitalism*, Durham, NC: Duke University Press.

Jancovich, Mark (1992) *Horror*, London: B.T. Batsford Ltd.

Jay, Paul (1984) *Being in the Text: Self-Representation from Wordsworth to Roland Barthes*, Ithaca, NY: Cornell University Press.

—— (1994) "Posing: Autobiography and the Subject of Photography," in Kathleen Ashley, Leigh Gilmore, and Gerald Peters (eds) *Autobiography and Postmodernism*, Amherst: University of Massachusetts Press.

Jeffrey, David Lyle (ed.) (1992) *A Dictionary of Biblical Tradition in English Literature*, Grand Rapids, MN: Wm. B. Eerdmans.

Jehl, Douglas (1997) "Babylon Journal: Look Who's Stealing Nebuchadnezzar's Thunder," *The New York Times*, July 2.

Jelinek, Estelle C. (ed.) (1980) *Women's Autobiography: Essays in Criticism*, Bloomington: Indiana University Press.

—— (1986) *The Tradition of Women's Autobiography: From Antiquity to the Present*, Boston, MA: Twayne.

Jeremias, Joachim (1964) "abussos," in Gerhard Kittel (ed.) *Theological Dictionary of the New Testament*, vol. I, Grand Rapids, MN: Wm. B. Eerdmans Publishing Company.

Johnson, Barbara (1987) "My Monster/My Self," in Harold Bloom (ed.) *Mary Shelley's Frankenstein*, New York: Chelsea House Publishers.

Johnston, E.B. (1982) "Jezebel," in Geoffrey W. Bromiley (ed.) *The International Standard Bible Encyclopedia*, Grand Rapids, MN: Wm. B. Eerdmans.

Jouve, Nicole Ward (1991) *White Woman Speaks with Forked Tongue: Criticism as Autobiography*, New York: Routledge.

Kant, Immanuel (1987) *Critique of Judgment*, trans. Werner S. Pluhar, Indianapolis: Hackett Publishing Company.

Kappeler, Susanne (1986) *The Pornography of Representation*, Minneapolis: University of Minnesota Press.

Keller, Catherine (1996) *Apocalypse Then and Now: A Feminist Guide to the End of the World*, Boston, MA: Beacon.

Kendrick, Walter (1991) *The Thrill of Fear: 250 Years of Scary Entertainment*, New York: Grove Weidenfeld.

Kessler, Edward (1986) *Flannery O'Connor and the Language of Apocalypse*, Princeton, NJ: Princeton University Press.

Ketchin, Susan (1994) *The Christ-Haunted Landscape: Faith and Doubt in Southern Fiction*, Jackson: University Press of Mississippi.

King, Stephen (1983) *Danse Macabre*, New York: Berkeley Books.

—— (1991) *The Stand*, New York: New American Library.

Kingwell, Mark (1996) *Dreams of Millennium: Report from a Culture on the Brink*, Toronto: Viking.

Kittel, Gerhard and Gerhard Friedrich (1964–74) *Theological Dictionary of the New Testament*, 10 vols, Grand Rapids, MI: Wm. B. Eerdmans.

Kristeva, Julia (1975) *Revolution in Poetic Language*, trans. Margaret Waller, New York: Columbia University Press.

—— (1980) *Desire in Language: A Semiotic Approach to Literature and Art*, ed. L.S. Roudiez and trans. T. Gora, A. Jardine, and L.S. Roudiez, New York: Columbia University Press.

—— (1982) *Powers of Horror: An Essay on Abjection*, trans. S. Roudiez, New York: Columbia University Press.

Krondorfer, Bjorn (1996) "Introduction," in Bjorn Krondorfer (ed.) *Men's Bodies, Men's Gods: Male Identities in a (Post-)Christian Culture*, New York: New York University Press.

Lacan, Jacques (1977) *Ecrits: A Selection*, trans. Alan Sheridan, New York: Norton.

Lenzen, Dieter (1989) "Disappearing Adulthood: Childhood as Redemption," in Dietmar Kamper and Christoph Wulf (eds) *Looking Back on the End of the World*, trans. David Antal, New York: Semiotext(e).

Levertov, Denise (1987) "Poetry Reading," in Valerie Andrews, Robert Bosnak, and Karen Walter Goodwin (eds) *Facing Apocalypse*, Dallas, TX: Spring Publications.

Lindsay, Hal (1980) *The Late, Great Planet Earth*, Grand Rapids, MI: Zondervan.

Lipton, Eunice (1993) *Alias Olympia: A Woman's Search for Manet's Notorious Model and Her Own Desire*, New York: Scribner.

Lovecraft, Howard Phillips (1973) *Supernatural Horror in Literature*, New York: Dover Publications.

Lyotard, Jean-François (1978) "One of the Things at Stake in Women's Struggles," *Sub/Stance* 20: 9–17.

McCaffery, Larry (ed.) (1991) *Storming the Reality Studio: A Casebook of Cyberpunk and Postmodern Fiction*, Durham, NC: Duke University Press.

McDannell, Colleen (1995) *Material Christianity: Religion and Popular Culture in America*, New Haven, CT: Yale University Press.

McDannell, Colleen and Bernard Lang (1988) *Heaven: A History*, New Haven, CT: Yale University Press.

McDowall, H.M. (1924) *Jezebel: A Tragedy*, Oxford: Basil Blackwell.

McFague, Sallie (1993) *The Body of God: An Ecological Theory*, Minneapolis, MN: Fortress.

McRay, John R. (1986) "Abyss," in William H. Grentz (ed.) *The Dictionary of Bible and Religion*, Nashville, TN: Abingdon Press.

Maguire, Matthew (1993) *The Tower*, Los Angeles, CA: Sun & Moon Press.

Magner, Denise (1997) "Apocalyptic Predictions and Millennial Fervor Attract Scholarly Notice," *The Chronicle for Higher Education* 44/9: A10–12.

Malbon, Elizabeth Struthers (1996) "The Literary Contexts of Mark 13," in Linda Bennett Elder, David L. Barr, and Elizabeth Struthers Malbon (eds) *Biblical and Humane: A Festschrift for John Priest*, Atlanta: Scholars Press.

Malina, Bruce (1981) *The New Testament World: Insights from Cultural Anthropology*, Atlanta, GA: John Knox Press.

Massé, Michelle A. (1992) *In the Name of Love: Women, Masochism, and the Gothic*, Ithaca, NY: Cornell University Press.

Massumi, Brian (ed.) (1993) *The Politics of Everyday Fear*, Minneapolis: University of Minnesota Press.

Miller, Nancy K. (1991) *Getting Personal: Feminist Occasions and Other Autobiographical Acts*, New York: Routledge.

Millett, Kate (1969) *Sexual Politics*, New York: Equinox Books.

Minkowski, Helmut (1991) *Vermutungen über den Turn zu Babel*, Freren: Luca Verlag.

Mitchell, W.J.T. (1986) *Iconology: Image, Text, Ideology*, Chicago, IL: University of Chicago Press.

—— (1994) *Picture Theory*, Chicago, IL: University of Chicago Press.

Modleski, Tania (1986) "The Terror of Pleasure: The Contemporary Horror Film and Postmodern Theory," in Tania Modleski (ed.) *Studies in Entertainment: Cultural Approaches to Mass Culture*, Bloomington: Indiana University Press.

Monteith, Moira (1986) *Women's Writing: A Challenge to Theory*, New York: St Martin's Press.

Moore, Stephen D. (1992) *Mark and Luke in Poststructuralist Perspective: Jesus Begins to Write*, New Haven, CT: Yale University Press.

—— (1996) *God's Gym*, London/New York: Routledge.

Moretti, Franco (1988) *Signs Taken for Wonders: Essays in the Sociology of Literary Forms*, trans. Susan Fischer, David Forgacs, and David Miller, London: Verso.

Morgan, David (1998) *Visual Piety: A History and Theory of Popular Religious Images*, Berkeley: University of California Press.

Morgan, Thais E. (1985) "Is There an Intertext in this Text?: Literary and Interdisciplinary Approaches to Intertextuality," *American Journal of Semiotics* 3(4): 1–40.

Morrow, James (1986) *This Is the Way the World Ends*, New York: Harcourt Brace.

—— (1990) *Only Begotten Daughter*, New York: Harcourt Brace.

—— (1996) "Bible Stories for Adults No. 20: The Tower," in *Bible Stories for Adults*, San Diego, CA: Harcourt Brace.

Morton, Patricia (1991) *Disfigured Images: The Historical Assault on Afro-American Women*, New York: Greenwood.

Myers, Ched (1988) *Binding the Strong Man: A Political Reading of Mark's Story of Jesus*, Maryknoll, NY: Orbis Books.

Naipaul, V.S. (1989) *A Turn in the South*, New York: Alfred A. Knopf.

Nietzsche, Friedrich (1956 [1887]) *The Birth of Tragedy and the Genealogy of Morals*, trans. Francis Golffing, Garden City, NY: Doubleday.

—— (1961) *Thus Spoke Zarathustra*, trans. R.J. Hollingdale, New York: Penguin.

O'Brien, Geoffrey (1995) *The Phantom Empire*, New York: W.W. Norton & Co.

O'Connor, Flannery (1969) *Mystery and Manners*, ed. Sally and Robert Fitzgerald, New York: Farrar, Straus & Giroux.

—— (1982) *The Complete Stories of Flannery O'Connor*, New York: Farrar, Straus & Giroux.

Olney, James (1972) *Metaphors of Self: The Meaning of Autobiography*, Princeton, NJ: Princeton University Press.

—— (1980) *Autobiography: Essays Theoretical and Critical*, Princeton, NJ: Princeton University Press.

Otto, Rudolf (1978) *The Idea of the Holy: An Inquiry into the Non-Rational Factor in the Idea of the Divine and its Relation to the Rational*, trans. John W. Harvey, New York: Oxford University Press.

Park, A. Sung (1989) "Theology of Han (the Abyss of Pain)," *Quarterly Review* (spring): 48–62.

Payne, Robert (1960) *Hubris: A Study of Pride*, New York: Harper & Brothers.

Penzoldt, Peter (1965) *The Supernatural in Fiction*, New York: Humanities Press.

Pinedo, Isabel Cristina (1997) *Recreational Terror: Women and the Pleasures of Horror Film Viewing*, Albany, NY: State University of New York Press.

Pippin, Tina (1992) *Death and Desire: The Rhetoric of Gender in the Apocalypse of John*, Louisville, KY: Westminster/John Knox Press.

—— (1993) "Wisdom and Apocalyptic in the Apocalypse of John: Desiring Sophia," in Brandon Scott and Leo G. Perdue (eds) *In Search of Wisdom*, Louisville, KY: Westminster/John Knox Press.

Punter, David (1996a) *The Literature of Terror: A History of Gothic Fictions from 1765 to the Present Day: Volume 1: The Gothic Tradition*, New York: Longman.

—— (1996b) *The Literature of Terror: A History of Gothic Fictions from 1765 to the Present Day: Volume 2: The Modern Gothic*, New York: Longman.

Quinby, Lee (1994) *Anti-Apocalypse: Exercises in Genealogical Criticism*, Minneapolis: University of Minnesota Press.

—— (1997) "Coercive Purity: The Dangerous Promise of Apocalyptic Masculinity," in Charles B. Stozier and Michael Flynn (eds) *The Year 2000: Essays on the End*, New York: New York University Press.

Rabinowitz, Nancy Sorkin (1992) "Tragedy and the Politics of Containment," in Amy Richlin (ed.) *Pornography and Representation in Greece and Rome*, New York: Oxford University Press.

Rabkin, Eric S. (1976) *The Fantastic in Literature*, Princeton, NJ: Princeton University Press.

Reddish, Mitchell (ed.) (1990) *Apocalyptic Literature: A Reader*, Nashville, TN: Abingdon Press.

Richard, Pablo (1995) *Apocalypse: A People's Commentary on the Book of Revelation*, Maryknoll, NY: Orbis.

Richlin, Amy (1992) "Introduction," in Amy Richlin (ed.) *Pornography and Representation in Greece and Rome*, New York: Oxford University Press.

Ricoeur, Paul (1967) *The Symbolism of Evil*, trans. Emerson Buchanan, Boston, MA: Beacon Press.

Riffaterre, Michael (1990) "Compulsory Reader Response: The Intertextual Drive," in Michael Worton and Judith Still (eds) *Intertextuality: Theories and Practices*, Manchester: Manchester University Press.

Robbins, Tom (1990) *Skinny Legs and All*, New York: Bantam Books.

Roberts, Robin (1993) *A New Species: Gender and Science in Science Fiction*, Urbana: University of Illinois Press.

Ruether, Rosemary Radford (1994) *Gaia and God: An Ecofeminist Theology of Earth Healing*, San Francisco: HarperSan Francisco.

Ruf, Frederick J. (1991) *The Creation of Chaos: William James and the Stylistic Making of a Disorderly World*, Albany: State University of New York Press.

Said, Edward W. (1978) *Orientalism*, New York: Vintage.

Sargisson, Lucy (1996) *Contemporary Feminist Utopianism*, London/New York: Routledge.

Sartre, Jean-Paul (1962) *Sketch for a Theory of the Emotions*, London: Methuen.

Scarry, Elaine (1985) *The Body in Pain: The Making and Unmaking of the World*, New York: Oxford University Press.

Schlobin, Roger (1988) "Children of a Darker God: A Taxonomy of Deep Horror Fiction and Film and Their Mass Appeals," *Journal of the Fantastic in the Arts* 1: 25–50.

—— (1992) "Prototypic Horror: The Genre of the Book of Job," *Semeia* 60: 23–38.

Schneider, Kirk J. (1993) *Horror and the Holy: Wisdom-Teachings of the Monster Tale*, Chicago, IL: Open Court.

Schüssler Fiorenza, Elisabeth (1991) *Revelation: Vision of a Just World*, Minneapolis, MN: Fortress Press.

—— (1998) *Sharing her Word: Feminist Biblical Interpretation in Context*, Boston: Beacon Press.

Scorsese, Martin (dir.) (1988) *Last Temptation of Christ*, Universal City Studios Inc. and Cineplex Odeon Films Canada Inc.

Segrest, Mab (1994) *Memoirs of a Race Traitor*, Boston, MA: South End Press.

Serres, Michael (1995) *Genesis (Studies in Literature and Science)*, trans. Genevieve James, Ann Arbor: University of Michigan Press.

Shapiro, Gary (1995) *Earthwards: Robert Smithson and Art after Babel*, Berkeley, CA: University of California Press.

Skal, David J. (1993) *The Monster Show: A Cultural History of Horror*, New York: W.W. Norton.

Smith, Sidonie (1987) *A Poetics of Women's Autobiography: Marginality and the Fictions of Self-Representation*, Bloomington: Indiana University Press.

Smith, Sidonie and Julia Watson (eds) (1992) *De/Colonizing the Subject: The Politics of Gender in Women's Autobiography*, Minneapolis: University of Minnesota Press.

Smith, Theophus H. (1994) *Conjuring Culture: Biblical Formations of Black America*, New York: Oxford University Press.

Stallybrass, Peter and Allon White (1986) *The Politics and Poetics of Transgression*, Ithaca, NY: Cornell University Press.

Stanton, Elizabeth Cady (ed.) (1974) *The Woman's Bible*, Seattle, WA: Coalition Task Force on Women and Religion.

Steiner, George (1970) *Language and Silence: Essays on Language, Literature and the Inhuman*, New York: Atheneum.

Sternberg, Meir (1985) *The Poetics of Biblical Narrative: Ideological Literature and the Drama of Reading*, Bloomington: Indiana University Press.

Stozier, Charles B. (1994) *Apocalypse: On the Psychology of Fundamentalism in America*, Boston, MA: Beacon Press.

Styron, William (1990) *Darkness Visible*, New York: Vintage.

Suleiman, Susan Rubin (1990) *Subversive Intent: Gender, Politics, and the Avant-Garde*, Cambridge, MA: Harvard University Press.

Sullivan, Jack (ed.) (1986) *The Penguin Encyclopedia of Horror and the Supernatural*, New York: Viking.

Sweeney, S.J. and Carol Singley (eds) (1993) *Anxious Power: Reading, Writing, and Ambivalence in Narrative by Women*, Albany: State University of New York Press.

Tabor, James D. and Eugene V. Gallagher (1995) *Why Waco? Cults and the Battle for Religious Freedom in America*, Berkeley: University of California Press.

Tartar, Maria (1992) *Off with Their Heads!: Fairy Tales and the Culture of Childhood*, Princeton, NJ: Princeton University Press.

Thibault, Paul (1991) *Social Semiotics as Praxis*, Minneapolis: University of Minnesota Press.

Thompson, Leonard L. (1990) *The Book of Revelation: Apocalypse and Empire*, New York: Oxford University Press.

Todorov, Tzvetan (1973) *The Fantastic: A Structural Approach to a Literary Genre*, Ithaca, NY: Cornell University Press.

Tolbert, Mary Ann (1995a) "Reading for Liberation," in Fernando F. Segovia and Mary Ann Tolbert (eds) *Reading from this Place: Volume 1: Social Location and Biblical Interpretation in the United States*, Minneapolis, MN: Fortress.

—— (1995b) "When Resistance Becomes Repression: Mark 13: 9–27 and the Poetics of Location," in Fernando F. Segovia and Mary Ann Tolbert (eds) *Reading from this Place: Volume 2: Social Location and Biblical Interpretation in Global Perspective*, Minneapolis, MN: Fortress.

Tolkin, Michael (dir.) (1991) *The Rapture*, New Line Cinema.

Twitchell, J. (1985) *Dreadful Pleasures: An Anatomy of Modern Horror*, New York: Oxford University Press.

Tymm, Marshall B. (1981) *Horror Literature: A Core Collection and Reference Guide*, New York: R.R. Bowker Company.

van der Meer, Frederick (1978) *Apocalypse: Visions from the Book of Revelation in Western Art*, London: Thames & Hudson.

Verhey, Allen (1984) *The Great Reversal: Ethics and the New Testament*, Grand Rapids, MN: Wm. B. Eerdmans.

Via, Dan O., Jr (1985) *The Ethics of Mark's Gospel in the Middle of Time*, Philadelphia, PA: Fortress.

Walker, Alice (1993a) *Possessing the Secret of Joy*, New York: Pocket Books.

—— (1993b) *Warrior Marks: Female Genital Mutilation and the Sexual Blinding of Women*, New York: Harcourt Brace.

Walker, Dorothy Clarke (1955) *Jezebel*, New York: McGraw-Hill Book Company.

Watson, Stephen H. (1985) "Abysses," in Hugh J. Silverman and Don Ihde (eds) *Hermeneutics and Deconstruction*, Albany: State University of New York Press.

Weiner, Sarah Elliston (1985) "The Tower of Babel in Netherlandish Painting," unpublished PhD dissertation, Columbia University, New York.

Weisberg, David B. (1985) "Fear of the Lord," in Paul J. Achtemeier (ed.) *Harper's Bible Dictionary*, San Francisco, CA: HarperSanFrancisco.

Weiskel, Thomas (1976) *The Romantic Sublime: Studies in the Structure and Psychology of Transcendence*, Baltimore, MD: The Johns Hopkins University Press.

White, Deborah Gray (1985) *Aren't I a Woman? Female Slaves in the Plantation South*, New York: W.W. Norton.

Wickham, Glynne (1987) *The Medieval Theatre*, New York: Cambridge University Press.

Winter, Douglas E. (1985) *Faces of Fear: Encounters with the Creators of Modern Horror*, New York: Berkley Books.

Wittig, Monique (1971) *Les Guérillères*, trans. David Le Vay, London: David Owen.

—— (1992) *The Straight Mind and Other Essays*, Boston, MA: Beacon Press.

Wolfe, Margaret Ripley (1995) *Daughters of Canaan: A Saga of Southern Women*, Lexington: University of Kentucky Press.

Wolstenholme, Susan (1993) *Gothic (Re)Visions: Writing Women as Readers* Albany: State University of New York Press.

Wood, Ralph (1988) *The Comedy of Redemption: Christian Faith and Comic Vision in Four American Novelists*, Notre Dame, IN: University of Notre Dame Press.

Woodward, Kenneth J. (1995) "Do We Need Satan?" *Newsweek*, November 13: 62–8.

Young, Dudley (1991) *Origins of the Sacred: The Ecstasies of Love and War*, New York: St Martin's Press.

Zinsser, William (ed.) (1987) *Inventing the Truth: The Art and Craft of Memoir*, Boston, MA: Houghton.

Zipes, Jack (1988) *Fairy Tales and the Art of Subversion: the Classical Genre for Children and the Process of Civilization*, New York: Methuen.

—— (1998) "Preface," in Tina Pippin and George Aichele (eds) *Violence, Utopia, and the Kingdom of God*, London: Routledge.

Žižek, Slavoj (1991) *For They Know Not What They Do: Enjoyment as a Political Factor*, New York: Verso.

—— (1994a) *The Metastases of Enjoyment: Six Essays on Woman and Causality*, New York: Verso.

—— (1994b) "How Did Marx Invent the Symptom?" in Slavoj Žižek (ed.) *Mapping Ideology*, London: Verso.

—— (1996) "'I Hear You with My Eyes'; or, the Invisible Master," in Renata Saleci and Slavoj Žižek (eds) *Gaze and Voice as Love Objects*, Durham, NC: Duke University Press.

—— (1997) *The Plague of Fantasies*, London/New York: Verso.

Zweig, C. and J. Abrams (1991) *Meeting the Shadow: The Hidden Power of the Dark Side of Human Nature*, Los Angeles, CA: Tarcher.

INDEX OF NAMES AND TERMS

INDEX OF BIBLICAL AND RELATED TEXTS